DESIGNING WITH

BULBS

THE JOY OF GARDENING

DESIGNING WITH

BULBS

BY RICHARD ROSENFELD

PHOTOGRAPHS BY JERRY HARPUR AND MARCUS HARPUR

COURAGE BOOKS

AN IMPRINT OF RUNNING PRESS

PHILADELPHIA • LONDON

Senior designer	Ashley Western
Designer	Peter Jackson
Senior editor	Annabel Morgan
Editor	Polly Boyd
Picture research	Mel Watson,
	Kate Brunt
Production controller	Patricia Harrington
Publishing director	Anne Ryland

© 1999 by Ryland Peters & Small

Printed and bound in China

Library of Congress Cataloging-in-Publication number
98–72366

ISBN 0-7624-0473-6

This edition published in the
United States in 1999 by
Courage Books, an imprint of
Running Press Book Publishers
125 South Twenty-second Street
Philadelphia, Pennsylvania
19103-4399

Visit us on the web!
www.runningpress.com

CONTENTS

Introduction

Bulbs are invaluable in the garden. With their glorious seasonal displays, they bring vitality and dynamism, complementing the more permanent plantings around them. The flowers of bulbous plants are highly prized by gardeners for their impressive range of colors—from subdued pastel tones to bold, splashy shades—as well as their diversity of form. Fortunately for the new gardener, bulbs are among the easiest of all garden plants to cultivate.

One of the main characteristics of bulbs is that they never fail to surprise. They seem to suddenly shoot up—some grow as much as twenty times their dormant height in just a matter of weeks—look magnificent in flower, and then disappear beneath the soil until the following season. They may be left to increase naturally, or alternatively—ideal where space is restricted—they may be lifted after flowering and replanted the following year, making room for other seasonal plants. Bulbs are great survivors:

Above: **A lively, striking clump of** *Lilium* **'Sterling Star'. Good from a distance, they are even better when viewed close up. The satiny, off-white petals are peppered with fine brown dots.**

Right: **Bulbs give gardens extra spin, especially the exotic-looking cannas (center) with their striking, tactile leaves and bright flowers. Embellish the scene with equally colorful lilies.**

some tolerate damp, others excessively dry conditions. Their resilience enables an immense variety to thrive, and indeed flourish, in gardens outside their natural habitat.

There is a vast range of bulbs to choose from, and the selection is continually expanding as breeders keep adding new and exciting scientific breakthroughs: tetraploid hybrid lilies, for example, now have 48 instead of 24 chromosomes, producing lilies with up to 150 blooms per stem. Garden centers sell tried and tested plants, but for more variety, browse through the catalogs of two or three bulb suppliers with a lively general range. If you are really bitten by the bulb bug, you may wish to turn to specialized catalogs, which include many rarities as well as the latest finds. It is well worth experimenting with new and unusual plants: the results can be particularly rewarding.

Bulbs may be planted in devoted beds, at the front of a perennial border with other plants, under trees or shrubs for winter flowering, in rock gardens, or in containers. They can also be naturalized in grass (see page 26), where they can multiply freely. Let the grass grow long while the bulb's foliage fades, storing energy for next year's display. If you mow the grass prematurely, there will be fewer, if any, flowers the following year.

Generally, most bulbs prefer a sunny site, hot dry summers, and good drainage, although many are perfectly happy in light shade or moist sites. Bear in mind that bulbs thrive in conditions that resemble those of their native habitat. If you want to try growing really tricky bulbs, you may need to invest in an alpine house. This is a special isolation unit—basically an unheated, well-ventilated glasshouse—that seals out the wet, creating a cold, dry environment. A greenhouse is a less expensive option, but at least 20 percent of the side panels must be converted to ventilators. Bulbs that flower well in summer but suffer during the winter from frost or wet may be grown as annuals.

For those with a tiny yard, or even no garden at all, there are numerous bulbs that can be grown in containers. In spring, scented hyacinths and daffodils bring a welcome splash of color to a patio or balcony, followed by lilies and cannas in summer, nerines and kaffir lilies in autumn, and *Cyclamen coum* in winter. Pots, windowboxes, barrels, sinks, or troughs all make attractive containers for bulbs, provided they have drainage holes in the base.

In the following chapters you will encounter both old favorites and recommendations for more unusual and exotic bulbs. Experiment with those that take your fancy, and plant them

One of the main characteristics of bulbs is that they never fail to surprise.

where you will most enjoy their sensational colors, forms, and scents. Although this book is organized by season, it is important to remember that predicting exactly when bulbs will appear is impossible. The seasons vary, as do other conditions. As a general guide, though, the following chapter divisions do apply. The designation "fully hardy" means bulbs can survive to 5°F (-15°C), "frost hardy" to 23°F (–5°C), and "half hardy" to 32°F (0°C).

Far left: **A spring blanket of white** *Anemone blanda*. **Liking dappled shade, they will quickly naturalize round tree trunks, and make an attractive combination with ornamental cherries or stately magnolias.**

Left: **A high-performance early summer border with a** good line-up of irises and alliums. The latter make a bold, punchy contribution to the garden, especially those with an intriguing drumstick shape—a ball of flowers atop a single slender stem.

Above: **Daffodils at their** informal best, massed sweeps naturalized in rough grass.

What is a bulb?

Bulbs are underground or soil-level storage organs. The term "bulb" generally refers to all bulbous plants, including corms, tubers, and rhizomes as well as true bulbs, although they are in fact botanically distinct. All bulbous plants store food that enables them to survive long periods of dormancy when the surface climate is hostile or unsuitable for growth, such as in a drought or during very cold weather. This dormant period can be crucial: it is often when next year's flowers form inside the bulb.

True bulbs are formed from modified leaves or leaf bases. Slice a typical bulb vertically in half, and you will find a protective tunic outside covering tightly packed scales that store food underneath, then the embryo stem, with the future leaves and flowers packed tightly in the center. At the bottom of the bulb is the basal plate, from which the roots grow. There are, of course, exceptions to the rule. Lilies do not have a protective covering, and lily scales can be easily removed.

Corms—crocuses and gladioli, for example—look similar to bulbs and are formed from the swollen base of last year's stem. This is usually replaced annually by a new corm which, for a brief period, co-exists with the old before it withers away. The tunics tend to be papery or fibrous, and there are no scales. Tubers are formed from swollen stem tissue that is used to store food; they do not have scales. Most tubers have surface "eyes," or buds (for example, cyclamen), that become new shoots. However, dahlias are an exception—they have no eyes. Rhizomes, such as some irises, are swollen modified stems that grow just beneath the surface of the soil. They resemble elongated corms, and creep horizontally through the soil by cell division at the growth points.

The easiest bulbs to grow are those whose growing needs match the conditions that exist in your yard, so check on a plant's individual requirements before buying. Purchase bulbs as soon as they are put on sale. Popular varieties sell out quickly, and if buying is delayed, bulbs may deteriorate. Spring bulbs become available in late summer and autumn, summer and autumn bulbs in spring (usually for planting after the last frost), and winter ones in the fall. Make sure the bulbs you buy have not been plundered from the wild: many now are labeled "from cultivated stock" to guarantee that they are environmentally friendly.

Bulbs can be bought ready-packed in their dormant state in garden centers, but if they have come into contact with any source of heat, there is a danger that premature growth might have been triggered. Bulbs sold loose in boxes are much easier to inspect: examine each one individually, and choose those that feel firm and heavy, rejecting any that are soft, hollow, or have started into growth. You should also discard any with scars, blemishes, and signs of mold or pest attack. It is generally best to plant bulbs immediately, before active growth begins, although delays are possible in some cases. Tulips for fall planting, for example, need not be planted until early or mid-winter, provided the ground is not too hard. Unplanted bulbs should always be stored in a cool, dry, dark place. For more details on planting and caring for bulbs, turn to page 76.

Left: **Three kinds of spring bulbs: cormous (the yellow crocus), bulbous (white snowdrop) and tuberous (purple cyclamen). Combine them in this way for a striking mix of colors.**

Above: **Mid-summer to autumn needn't be tame if you invest in plenty of dahlias. The spiky shapes of the cactus-flowered varieties, such as 'Hillcrest Royal', are particularly eyecatching.**

Right: **Naturalized in grass, daffodils and fritillaries create rich jewellike points of color and create a overall effect that is reminiscent of a medieval tapestry.**

Of all the seasons in the year, spring is the most exciting. It is the time of regeneration and new life, of anticipation and new beginnings. The leaves unfurl their new, lush green growth, and spring bulbs emerge from their underground chambers, bringing fresh, vibrant hues and tones to the garden.

SPRING

Daffodils

The bright, clear colors of daffodils are a welcome sight, signaling the arrival of spring. However, if you feel—like many—that daffodils have suffered from overexposure, read on. There are about 1,700 daffodils (*Narcissus*) available, divided into 12 botanical groups (the twelfth is a miscellaneous category). They offer a wide choice of colors: apricot, lemon, orange, pink, white, and, of course, yellow. There are also many different forms. *Narcissus triandrus*, with its reflexed petals and nodding head, resembles a fuchsia, while *N.* 'Broadway Star', with its bright orange stripes, is reminiscent of a comical lollipop. Heights range

from the tiny, delicate white *N. watieri*, a dainty 4 in (10 cm) high, to the knee-high *N.* 'Stratosphere', which reaches 26 in (65 cm). Many are deliciously scented, such as the heady *N.* × *odorus*.

A powerful blast of one variety or color of daffodil concentrated in a single area can look spectacular. Choose a stunner: the sweetly scented *N. poeticus* var. *recurvus* is a staggering beauty, with crisp white flowers and a sharp yellow

eye rimmed in red, 14 in (35 cm) high. *N.* 'Tête-à-Tête' is a prolific early, yellow, trumpet-shaped daffodil that grows to half the height. Alternatively, to create a whirling blur of color, combine two daffodils in different but harmonious shades, such as the lemon-white *N.* 'February Silver' and the rich yellow *N.* 'February Gold', both 12 in (30 cm) high. Other notable daffodils include *N. cyclamineus*, a small bright-yellow flower with swept-back segments and sprouting a long thin distinctive trumpet, carried on a slender stem 8 in (20 cm) high; *N.* 'Rip van Winkle', a miniature raggedy pompom of feathery yellow petals only 6 in (15 cm) high; and the late-flowering, extraordinary-looking, *N.* 'Tricollet', 15 in (38 cm) high, with six creamy petals and a bizarre, orange T-shaped marking on top.

Daffodils can be breathtaking if left to naturalize freely in grass, creating a bold swathe of color in spring. The fast-spreading *N. bulbocodium* is a good choice for this. Growing daffodils in grass could not be easier. Choose a sunny spot, then roll back the sod in the fall and plant the bulbs at one and a half to two times their depth and 8–12 in (20–30 cm) apart, allowing them space to multiply. Do not mow the grass around the bulbs for at least six weeks after flowering, to allow them to store up energy for next year's display.

Alternatively, you may prefer a more ordered display. Try growing four perfect segments of yellow at the corners of a square or rectangular lawn, and enjoy the sight from an upstairs window. But be warned—for displays that depend on an orderly, formal pattern, it is best not to use vigorous spreaders.

In smaller gardens, stick to bright, punchy clumps of daffodils in the flowerbed. Plant them between shrub roses; dot them next to blue hyacinths; merge them with early tulips; and scatter them among packs of blue *Anemone blanda*, magenta

Left: **Even if *Narcissus* 'February Gold' does not appear quite as early as its name promises, when it does flower its large trumpet and rich yellow shade will bring cheer to the spring garden.**

Right: **A mass of naturalized daffodils, in colors ranging from orange to white, create a vibrant, cheerful effect in spring. They will increase year by year if their foliage is allowed to die back naturally.**

A powerful blast of one kind or color of daffodil concentrated in a single area can look spectacular in the garden.

Left: *Narcissus* 'Actaea' flowers in late spring. Its flat, white flower and yellow cup have a fragile charm that is an appealing contrast to many of the larger narcissi.

Anemone blanda 'Radar', and bright blue *Scilla bifolia*. And to crown the groupings, plant them beneath one of the prettiest of spring-flowering shrubs, the white *Magnolia stellata*.

The pick of the scented daffodils are the deliciously fragrant late autumn- to mid-spring-flowering Tazettas, such as *N*. 'Geranium' and the exquisitely delicate paper whites, *N. papyraceus*. Equally sweetly scented are the mid- to late spring-

flowering Jonquils, such as *N*. 'Baby Moon' and *N*. 'Bobbysoxer'. Both kinds carry several clusters of small flowers on each stem and are excellent as cut flowers.

Some Tazettas are half-hardy, requiring a mild climate and sunny border, preferably in the shelter of a wall. In cooler climates, they can be grown in pots indoors to provide protection from frost. The paper whites, with their strong and delicious scent, are

Above: **There is a wide choice of companion plants for daffodils. Blue anemones contrast well with bright yellow flowers, or for a more unusual effect, try magenta** *Anemone blanda* 'Radar'.

particularly suitable for growing as potted plants. Plant them up in fall in loam-based potting medium with an extra 30 percent grit, 2in (5cm) deep and apart. Place the pots in a sunny spot, such as a windowsill, and within six weeks the bulbs will flower. Tazettas can be grown in glass vases filled with gravel or even colored marbles. Half-fill a vase with gravel and place the bulbs on top, then wedge them in place with more gravel. Add water to just below the base of the bulbs. Start the bulbs off in a cool shed or garage, at about 50°F (10°C), then transfer them indoors, at no more than 65°F (18°C), for flowering.

Jonquils are often bought in bud, since they require a considerable amount of maintenance in the early stages. However, they can also be grown in pots. Plant the bulbs in early autumn, then sink the pots in the ground, covered with 6–8 in (15–20 cm)

of composted bark. This provides the moisture, darkness, and constant temperature that the bulbs need for growth. Leave them for 16 weeks to allow the roots to grow, then transfer them to a well-ventilated shed, with a temperature of 45–50°F (7–10°C), watering when the soil is dry. When the buds open, bring the plants into the house. Do not bring them in any sooner, since heat will thwart the flowers.

Right: *Narcissus* 'Grand Soleil D'or' is a delicate Tazetta that can also be forced for a sweetly scented early indoor show. If grown outside, it needs a sheltered and frost-free spot in order to flower.

Above: **The fragrant *Narcissus papyraceus* can be grown indoors in pots for winter flowers or planted in the garden for a spring display. The bulbs like a good baking while they are dormant.**

Hyacinths

Of all the spring bulbs, hyacinths are probably the most sweetly fragrant. Many people think of them as pot plants, but they also put on a wonderful display in the garden. Almost all the hyacinths commonly available descend from *Hyacinthus orientalis*. There are approximately fifty cultivars to choose from in reds, pinks, yellows, lilacs, and blues. Particularly colorful blooms include *H. orientalis* 'Queen of the Violets', in a rich, vivid shade of purple, and *H. o.* 'Distinction', a deep beet-purple.

Plant hyacinths with the white-stemmed bramble *Rubus cockburnianus*, or the purple-blue sweet pea *Lathyrus vernus*. They are also wonderful combined with pale green *Helleborus orientalis*. Plant the bulbs in autumn, 5–6 in (13–15 cm) deep. The depth is vital: in shallower conditions, the flowers will diminish. When planting hyacinths in a pot, make sure their tips protrude through the bulb fiber. Keep them in the dark until the shoots are 2 in (5 cm) high, then bring them into the light.

Below: **Hyacinths are such popular indoor plants that it is easy to forget that the bulbs can be grown outside, where their heady scent is not quite as overwhelming. Combine with violas and bellis for a colorful display.**

Crocuses

Available in a vast choice of colors and attractive markings, crocuses are exquisite in a flowerbed, and you do not need a mass of them to make a statement. A small group can be a show-stopper. Try *Crocus corsicus*, which is lilac inside with jazzy orange styles and purple veining outside, or *C. angustifolius*, bronze with a yellow interior. Their small size means that crocuses can also be planted in rock gardens, as well as in nooks and crannies around the garden, where they will surprise and delight.

Crocuses are excellent for naturalizing. The early crocus, *C. tommasinianus*, is a popular choice, but can be invasive. *C. vernus* 'Pickwick' also makes terrific clumps. For a small area, choose *C. tommasinianus* 'Barr's Purple', which will not spread as quickly. Crocuses prefer a sunny site. Plant spring-flowering crocuses in autumn, and the autumn crocuses in late summer.

Above: **The wild *Crocus vernus* has fathered some excellent cultivars. The goblet-shaped white flowers of *C. v.* 'Pickwick' are streaked with deep purple and, being quick to multiply, will put on a strong spring display.**

Fritillaries

Immensely diverse, there are fritillaries to suit everyone: exotic and dramatic crown imperials; quieter kinds for the front of the bed or rock garden; and spreaders that will naturalize in grass.

Fritillaria imperialis, the stately crown imperial, with its 3 ft (90 cm) high stems, nodding cup-shaped flowers in yellow and orange, and its tufty green crown, falls into the exotic-looking category. Plant them in groups around trees, beside paths, or in large tubs. F. persica 'Adiyaman', with dark plum-colored flowers, reaches the same height. Grow it in a warm, sheltered spot.

The smaller species possess a subtle, delicate charm, largely due to their nodding heads and subtle yet exquisite patterning. F. michailovskyi, 8 in (20 cm) high, has nodding, bell-shaped

bicolored flowers, the top half yellow, the lower deepest maroon. Its dainty stature means it is well suited to the front of the border or rock garden, but be warned: it requires well-drained soil. F. pallidiflora, 18 in (45 cm) high, produces squared yellow bells dotted with red on the inside. It prefers cool, woodland conditions, but will tolerate most fertile soils. F. meleagris, the snake's head fritillary, is the best spreader and is ideal for naturalizing. It has dangling, fragile-looking checked purple-pink and white flowers, grows 10 in (25 cm) high, and thrives in heavy, damp soil.

Below: **From a distance, Fritillaria meleagris appears to be a modest, none-too- showy bulb. However, seen up close, its checked markings are quite exquisite.**

Tulips

To see how tulips should be grown, visit the garden of the French impressionist painter Claude Monet, at Giverny, north of Paris. After a visit to the Dutch tulip fields in 1886, he increasingly used these flowers in his compositions. "Enormous fields in full bloom," he said, "enough to drive a poor painter crazy." As a gardener, he started planting intense groupings of tulips in one color. Another fine display of tulips can be seen every year at the famous garden at Sissinghurst Castle in Kent, England; fresh, juicy, startling colors are massed together under two long rows of lime trees.

Tulips are suited to both formal and informal planting, and are available in almost every color imaginable. They can be brash, delicate, or clear in hue. Flowering generally takes place in mid- and late spring. Tulips are divided into 15 different botanical groupings, with six different flower shapes. You can either plant

Tulips are ideally suited to both formal and informal planting, and are available in almost every color imaginable.

them like Monet did—a huge, powerful block in a single plot—or have them running in packs through a perennial border. A vivid row of pots, each containing one kind and color of tulip, will also offer a simple but stunning display.

The Parrot tulips, with their crimped, ragged petals, often in brash colors, are generally the most fun and flamboyant of all the tulips. *Tulipa* 'Estella Rijnveld' has a color scheme that is reminiscent of raspberry ripple ice cream: the petals are marked with broad swirls of red and white. The exotic *T.* 'Flaming Parrot' is pale yellow patterned with stripes and streaks of crimson. The Viridifloras are another distinctive group. They are sometimes completely green, with colored edges, or another color marked with green bands or stripes. *T.* 'Spring Green', for example, has ivory-white flowers with lime-green markings, which pick up the fresh green of new spring growth.

One of the most striking of all tulips is the elegant Lily-flowered *Tulipa* 'White Triumphator', a white, goblet-shaped flower on a slender 2 ft (60 cm) high stem. Try it with the double *T.* 'Angélique', a clear pink, and blue forget-me-nots (*Myosotis*): a stunning combination. Other stunners include two Triumph group tulips, *T.* 'Attila', with gentle purple-violet flowers, and *T.* 'Shirley', with white and carmine flowers; and three Lily-flowered beauties, *T.* 'Burgundy', a rich wine shade; *T.* 'Maytime' with reddish violet blooms; and *T.* 'China Pink', with goblet-shaped clear pink flowers.

Choose companions for tulips carefully. The acid-green yellow-tipped *Euphorbia polychroma* 'Major', the warm reds yellows and oranges of wallflowers (*Erysimum*), low-growing blue or white forget-me-nots, starry-flowered sweet woodruff (*Galium odoratum*), dark green acanthus leaves, bright blue grape hyacinths (*Muscari*), and the feathery foliage of giant fennel (*Ferula*) all look sensational with tulips. For a chic and unusual black and white planting, plant the striking near-black tulip, *T.* 'Queen of Night', against the toothed, silvery leaves of cardoons (*Cynara cardunculus*), or white daisies.

Left: ***Tulipa praestans*** **'Fusilier', with its juicy orange flowers and elegant blue-green foliage, creates an exciting color contrast when grown next to zingy lime-green euphorbias.**

Above: **There may be tulips with more exciting flower shapes, but none can beat the wonderful intense purple shade of** *Tulipa* **'Queen of Night'. It adds a touch of sophistication to the border.**

When tulips have finished flowering, allow them to die down naturally until their growing cycle is finished. It is vital to remove the petals and foliage promptly afterward to prevent tulip fire disease (*see page* 77), and to lift them and replant them in new soil after two years on the same site. Store the lifted bulbs in a verminproof box in a cool, dry place until re-planting in late fall or early winter, and replace them with cannas, dahlias, and zinnias for the summer months. Avoid planting tulips too early, or they may shoot up, only to be killed by frost.

Above: **Tulips are classified in 15 different divisions, largely grouped by flower shape. The Lily-flowered group, which includes *T.* 'White Triumphator', is perhaps the most elegant of them all.**

Right: **If you have a spare patch of ground, think tulips. Massed together on their own in a single-plot planting, they will create a bold and beautiful block of color in the garden in late spring.**

Irises

The iris is one of the most exquisite of all spring bulbs. The larger cultivars flower in summer, so are featured in the next chapter (*see page* 40), but there are many beautiful spring-flowering varieties.

The bulbous Juno irises, 2–24 in (5–60 cm) high, appear in early spring. Most prefer dry hot ground and well-drained soil, and are ideal for the rock garden, although a few prefer damp conditions. Many Juno bulbs are very difficult to grow, so it is best to stick to the trio listed here. *Iris cycloglossa*, 18 in (45 cm) high, is lilac with yellow and white markings and tolerates some damp; *I. magnifica* is taller, at 2 ft (60 cm), and has lilac petals with white and yellow markings; and the beautiful *I. bucharica*, 12 in (30 cm) high, has white to lemon-yellow flowers with golden falls

Above: **The intermediate bearded** *Iris* **'Miss Carla' has subtle coloring and papery petals with ruffled edges.** **Plant it close to the front of the flowerbed, where its understated elegance can be fully appreciated.**

There are also some gorgeous new cultivars, such as Iris 'Arnold Sunrise', with white and yellow flowers.

(or outer petals). It prefers lime and a dry site, but will also tolerate damper soil. All three are susceptible to attacks from slugs. The Crested Irises also flower in mid- to late spring, but are equally difficult to grow. However, *I. japonica* 'Ledger's Variety', in white and yellow, is easier than most.

Bearded irises flower in mid- to late spring. These irises are rhizomatous, rather than bulbous, and have distinctive swordlike foliage and flowers with a "beard"—a small group of fluffy hairs on the falls. They are grouped botanically by height. The standard dwarf bearded irises, hardy and easy to grow, flower earliest, in mid-spring, and reach 8–16 in (20–40 cm) in height. Try the cream *Iris* 'Bibury' or white and violet *I.* 'Boo'. The miniatures, no higher than 8 in (20 cm), are ideal for rock gardens, where the purple *I.* 'Grapelet' looks spectacular teamed with *I.* 'Knick Knack', which is white with delicate blue veining.

The intermediate bearded irises, reaching 16–28 in (40–70 cm) in height, flower at the end of spring. They include *Iris* 'Raspberry Blush', in bright raspberry pink; *I.* 'Langport Phoenix', in sky blue with violet; and *I.* 'Miss Carla', in pale blue and white.

The Pacific coast irises are a group of beardless irises that also flower in mid- and late spring. *I. douglasiana*, 2 ft (60 cm) high, with veined, lilac flowers, is one of the best. There are also some gorgeous new cultivars, such as *I.* 'Arnold Sunrise', 10 in (25 cm) high, which has white flowers with a bright yellow patch.

Above: **Like most bearded rhizomatous irises, *Iris* 'Raspberry Blush' demands a bright, sunny position in fertile soil where it can dry out but won't get frazzled during the summer.**

Far left: **The British nursery Kelways, in Langport, Somerset, developed the 'Langport' series of intermediate bearded irises. 'Langport Wren' is a 1995 introduction, in an unusual magenta–brown shade.**

Left: ***Iris* 'Lake Kenke' has extravagantly ruffled purple-lilac flowers that add glamor to the spring yard.**

SPRING GALLERY

Anemone blanda

Height: 6 in (15 cm), spread: 6 in (15 cm); flowers in spring; fully hardy

Attractive tuberous perennial producing a large flush of solitary saucer-shaped flowers in violet, blue, pink, magenta, or white. Prefers well-drained, fertile soil in full sun, but will tolerate light shade. Excellent for naturalizing.

Arisaema griffithii

Height: 20 in (50 cm), spread: 6 in (15 cm); flowers in late spring to early summer; half hardy

Dramatic tuberous perennial with a hood-like purple spathe, 6 in (15 cm) long. Grow in fertile, moist soil in light shade. In cool climates, overwinter in a cool greenhouse. Good in a border.

Arisarum proboscideum

Height: 6 in (15 cm), spread: 10 in (25 cm); flowers in late spring to early summer; fully hardy

Rhizomatous perennial grown for its hooded chocolate-brown spathes, 1½ in (4 cm) long, each with a curious mouselike tail. Requires fertile soil in partial shade. Good for a bed, rock garden, or woodland garden.

Arum dioscoridis

Height: 14 in (35 cm), spread 6 in (15 cm); flowers in spring; frost hardy

Tuberous perennial with a dramatic dark, spathelike purple or pale green hood, 10 in (25 cm) long, spotted with dark maroon blotches. Requires a warm, sunny position with well-drained, fertile soil.

Chionodoxa sardensis
(Glory of the snow)

Height: 6 in (15 cm), spread: 1½ in (3.5 cm); flowers in early spring; fully hardy

Small, bulbous perennial bearing rich blue, star-shaped flowers with blue centers. Needs well-drained soil in full sun, but avoid heat and aridity. Grows well beneath shrubs and trees or in a rock garden.

Crocus tommasinianus

Height: 4 in (10 cm), spread: 1 in (2.5 cm); flowers in late winter to spring; fully hardy

Vigorous cormous perennial with pale lilac to purple-red flowers. Requires full sun, moderately fertile ground, and good drainage. An invasive naturalizer in grass.

Erythronium
(Dog's-tooth violet, trout lily)

Height: 3–12 in (8–30 cm), spread : 3–14 in (8–35 cm); flowers in spring to early summer; fully hardy

Clump-forming bulbous perennials, many, such as Erythronium dens-canis, with distinctive, mottled foliage. Usually white, yellow, pink, or violet in color. Need moist, shady sites with fertile, well-drained, acid soil. Dislike hot sun. Good for cut flowers.

Fritillaria (Fritillary)

Height: 3–39 in (8 cm–1 m), spread: 2–12 in (5–30 cm); flowers spring to early summer; fully hardy

Striking bulbous perennials with nodding plum to orange to white bell-shaped flowers, some bicolored (F. michailovskyi), others checked (F. latifolia). Fritillaries are divided into four cultivation groups: the first requires fertile, sharply drained soil and full sun; the second dry, moderately fertile soil and full sun; third, woodland species prefer damp, humus-rich soil in sun to light shade; and finally wet-intolerant species need the protection of an alpine house. Good for rock gardens, beds, containers, and cut flowers.

Galanthus (Snowdrop)

Height: 4–10 in (10–25 cm), spread: 2–3 in (5–8 cm); flowers in late winter to spring; mostly fully hardy

Easy-to-grow bulbous perennials with white flowers marked in green. Require light shade and moist, fertile soil. Dislike hot sun. Divide and replant after flowering. Excellent for naturalizing and make good cut flowers.

Hyacinthoides hispanica
(Spanish bluebell)

Height: 16 in (40 cm), spread 4 in (10 cm); flowers in spring; fully hardy

Scented bulbous perennial with tiny flowers held on a single stem. Colors range from dark blue to pink and white. Needs well-drained soil in sun or light shade. Dislikes hot sun. Ideal for naturalizing.

Top left:
***Anemone blanda* 'White Splendour'**

Top right:
Chionodoxa sardensis

Far left:
Fritillaria imperialis

Above center:
Crocus tommasinianus

Above:
Erythronium dens-canis

Left:
***Galanthus* 'Merlin'**

Opposite page:
***Anemone nemorosa* 'Robinsoniana'**

Opposite: ***Hyacinthus orientalis 'Carnegie'***; Left: ***Ornithogalum nutans;*** Below: ***Muscari armeniacum 'Early Giant'***

others demand alkaline soil (the Jonquils and Tazettas). Ideal for naturalizing, growing in the border, containers, and cut flowers.

Ornithogalum nutans (Star-of-Bethlehem)

Height: 8–24 in (20–60 cm), spread 2 in (5 cm); flowers in spring; fully hardy

Bulbous perennial with nodding, silvery white flowers and a gray-green stripe on the outside of the petals. Requires well-drained soil in full sun or light shade.

Tulipa (Tulip)

Height: 6–24 in (15–60 cm), spread: 4–8 in (10–20 cm); flower in mid- to late spring; fully hardy

Distinctive bulbous perennials in a vast range of colors, shapes, and heights. A well-drained soil is essential. They dislike the wet, and prefer alkaline soil. Will put on an excellent spring show in beds and containers, and make good cut flowers.

Hyacinthus orientalis (Hyacinth)

Height: 10 in (25 cm), spread: 3 in (8 cm); flowers in early spring; fully hardy

Bulbous perennial with highly fragrant tubular, bell-shaped, waxy flowers held on a central spike. Colors include blue, pink, and yellow. Requires well-drained soil in sun or dappled shade. Suitable for beds, containers, and cut flowers.

Iris species and cultivars (Bearded irises)

Height: 2–28 in (5–70 cm), spread: 6–24 in (15–60 cm); flowers in mid-spring to early summer; fully hardy

Attractive rhizomatous perennials with distinctive fans of upright, strap-shaped leaves and large flowers, with a hairy "beard" on the falls, in violet, purple, white, and yellow. Require well-drained, neutral to slightly acid, fertile soil in full sun. Will not tolerate winter wet. Good for small gardens.

Muscari (Grape hyacinth)

Height: 4–8 in (10–20 cm), spread: 2 in (5 cm); flowers in spring or occasionally autumn; fully hardy

Small bulbous perennials with blue, white, or yellow flowers of varying shapes. One of the most reliable is the bright blue *M. armeniacum*, which has stout spikes densely covered with tiny bell-shaped

flowers. Require well-drained soil in full sun. A good filler at the front of a mixed bed and also suitable for naturalizing. Some species are delicately scented.

Narcissus (Daffodil)

Height: 4–20 in (10–50 cm), spread: 2–6 in (5–16 cm); flowers in spring, sometimes autumn or winter; mostly fully hardy

Variable bulbous perennials, some highly scented, available in a wide range of colors and shapes, but all with a trumpetlike corona at the center of the flower. Grow in an open, sunny site in moist, well-drained soil. Some prefer slightly acid conditions (*N. cyclamineus* and *N. bulbocodium*),

Gardeners are spoiled for choice in the summer. The range of bulbs available is immense, and the color palette is exciting and varied; including dazzling, sunny shades as well as rich, deep tones. Fragrant and exotic, summer bulbs are guaranteed to give a garden an extra slice of "oomph."

SUMMER

Architectural plants

Many summer bulbs are grown for their architectural qualities: strong in form, these plants strike a bold or dramatic note in a garden. Alliums, or ornamental onions, are excellent architectural summer plants, and are also easy to grow. Drumsticklike in shape, they have lilac or purple ball-shaped flowerheads, up to 8 in (20 cm) in diameter, topping lofty stems, 18 in (45 cm) high or taller. The eyecatching flowerheads consist of scores of tiny, star-shaped flowers. In mid-summer, most alliums shed their flowers and engage the eye with their "scaffolding": a pompom of trembling, radiating prongs with green pods at the tips.

Alliums need a showbizzy setting. In Rosemary Verey's garden at Barnsley House, Gloucestershire, England, they look spectacular growing under a laburnum arch. In early summer, the arch is ablaze with yellow and purple: the flowers of *Laburnum* × *watereri* 'Vossii' hang down in thickets, and jabbing straight up toward them are hundreds of puffy, round violet heads of

Allium aflatunense, carried on thin green stalks 4 ft (1.2 m) high. The effect is that of a magical, two-toned tunnel. Other alliums to try include the metallic lilac *A. cristophii* and the sky-blue *A. caeruleum*, both 2 ft (60 cm) high, and a pair of blockbusters: the purple *A. giganteum*, 4 ft (1.2 m) high, and the slightly taller lilac-purple *A.* 'Globemaster'. Grow them around red and white metal rods placed in gravel beds, or beside grasses like the golden yellow *Milium effusum* 'Aureum', 2 ft (60 cm) high.

Related to the alliums and flowering in early summer, *Nectaroscordum siculum* and *N.* subsp. *bulgaricum* are best viewed close up. They both have thin, vertical stems topped with loose clusters of downward-facing, bell-shaped flowers. *N. siculum* has creamy white flowers, with a green and purple tinge, borne on 3 ft (90 cm) stems, while those of *N. s.* subsp. *bulgaricum* are much flashier, in white patterned with red and green. Like alliums, the leaves of both smell strongly of garlic if crushed. Both thrive in bright sun or light shade, and tolerate even quite heavy soil. Plant them wherever you find space in your garden: in gaps between shrubs—they look particularly effective with pyracanthas—or growing through boxwood (*Buxus*). *Nectaroscordum* also make wonderful dried flowers.

Among the most striking of summer plants are the rhizomatous kniphofias, or red-hot pokers. They send up straight spikes, 1–6 ft (30 cm–1.8 m) high, topped with brightly colored, bottlebrushlike flowerheads. The flowers of some cultivars dramatically turn color from bright red to sharp yellow, so flowerheads may be bicolored, the top half red, the lower half yellow. *Kniphofia caulescens* (red fading to yellow), *K.* 'Royal Standard' (red buds with yellow flowers), and *K.* 'Sunningdale Yellow' (yellow) are the pick of the bunch, with *K. triangularis* (orange-red) flowering in early autumn to prolong the display. Kniphofias look good with other tall, thin plants, such as mulleins (*Verbascum*), teasels (*Dipsacus*), and the open-branching *Cynara cardunculus*. As with most bulbous perennials, never grow one kniphofia by itself: they look far more effective in bold clusters.

For mid- and late-summer impact, big, blowsy gladioli (*Gladiolus*) are hard to beat. Although they can be hard to grow, their tall, elegant forms are worth the effort. Among the best are *Gladiolus* 'Elvira', 32 in (80 cm) high, bearing white flowers with red, kiss-like markings on the petals; *G.* 'Mi Mi', 4 ft (1.2 m) high,

with lavender and white flowers; and *G.* 'Green Woodpecker', 5 ft (1.5 m) high, in red and lemon. Prolong the show by planting them at 10-day intervals in spring. Gladioli look particularly effective packed in bays in the border, or puncturing a big, white puffy cloud of *Gypsophila paniculata*, which grows about 4 ft (1.2 m) high. They are also suited to a cottage garden: combine them with penstemons, old roses, clematis, and a purple *Verbena bonariensis*. Gladioli make excellent cut flowers. Cut when in bud, leaving 6 in (15 cm) of stem beneath the last flower.

Late summer also brings other surprises. *Dierama pulcherrimum*, the angel's fishing rod, has loose, airy, arching stems 4ft (1.2 m) high, covered with lipstick-pink flowers. A terrific convention-breaker, it looks wonderful sitting at the front of a planting scheme rather than in the middle of a bed, as its size would suggest. Dierama can also soften formal topiary, sprouting out of a circle of boxwood (*Buxus*) or arching over rounded shrubs like *Hebe rakaiensis*. Or try it dangling over a pond, where the water will reflect its graceful habit.

Far left: **If you only grow one bulb, this should be it— *Allium cristophii*. A melon-sized ball of thousands of tiny flowers giving a silvery, shiny scaffolded effect atop a sturdy, straight stem. Makes excellent cut flowers.**

Left: **Intriguing and graceful, *Nectaroscordum siculum* subsp. *bulgaricum* adds style to the border. The flowers sit on lofty 4 ft (1.2 m) stems, and look good reflected in an adjacent pond.**

Right: **The classic, two-tone combination of purple drumstick alliums beneath** **a flash of yellow laburnum in Rosemary Verey's garden at Barnsley House, England.**

Colorful flowers

Alstroemerias should head any list of essential summer flowers. Traditionally listed as perennials, they actually have rhizomelike tubers. Alstromerias look so exotic that you might think a high-tech conservatory was necessary to grow them. Not so.

The latest range of alstroemerias, the Princess Hybrids—such as *Alstroemeria* 'Princess Grace' and *A*. 'Princess Alice'—are among the most important new flowers of the last fifty years or so. Flower colors include white, pink, orange, and yellow. The Princess Hybrids flower for a good five months throughout summer to autumn, and the cut flowers last between three to four weeks. The Princess Hybrids like plenty of sun and moist, well-drained soil. Although they are extremely hardy, it is prudent to give a thick, frost-protective mulch in the first winter. The Princesses reach about 3 ft (90 cm)—if you need something smaller, the 'Little Princess' series grow to about 15 in (38 cm).

The *Alstroemeria* Ligtu Hybrids come in a wide color range, and self-seed to form big, bold groups. The warm, clear pinks mix and match with softer colors, tone down hot reds, and clash with yellows. If you prefer a fiery blast of orange, try *Alstroemeria aurea*, a determined spreader that looks good popping up through other plants, especially *Helianthemum* 'Fire Dragon', 12 in (30 cm) high.

Crocosmias, with their funnel-shaped flowers in bold shades of orange, orange-red, and yellow, shriek like parrots in mid- and late summer. *C*. 'Firebird', one of the most striking, is tomato-red with a yellow throat. Grow them among tall, grass-like foliage, such as *Acanthus spinosus*, 4 ft (1.2 m) high, or with wispy grasses. Alternatively, try them under the gigantic arms of *Onopordum nervosum*, which grows 9 ft (2.7 m) high and has purple, thistlelike flowers. Set them against the bright red *Chrysanthemum* 'Pennine Signal', 4 ft (1.2 m) high, or alongside the lilac blue of *Campanula lactiflora*, 4 ft (1.2 m) high.

Right: **In late summer, gardens can sometimes look a little tired and faded. This will not be the case, however, if you** plant the stunning *Crocosmia* **'Emily Mackenzie', which combines colorful blooms with straplike, shiny foliage.**

Top: The *Alstroemeria* Ligtu Hybrids come in a wide color range of strong corals, oranges, terracottas, and other fiery hues, as well as softer, more subtle shades of pink, yellow, and cream.

Above: The typical markings of *Alstroemeria*—showy, satiny petals patterned with striking dots and dashes of color. Indispensable as a cut flower, and for bringing a slice of exotica to the border.

The magenta *Gladiolus communis* subsp. *byzantinus* provides another shock of summer color. It is hardier and more vigorous than the other gladioli, and grows to 3 ft (90 cm). Even in severe winters, you can leave it in the ground with a protective mulch. Good companions are the tall magenta *Geranium psilostemon*, 3 ft (90 cm) high, and *Yucca filamentosa*, a serious plant for a hot position, with stiff, strap-shaped leaves and scores of scented, creamy white flowers on stems 6½ft (2 m) high. Alternatively, grow it in a free-flow of poppies (*Papaver*), foxgloves (*Digitalis*), campanulas, evening primrose (*Oenothera*), columbines (*Aquilegia*), and bulbous camassias, especially the rich blue *Camassia leichtlinii* 'Electra', 3 ft (90 cm) high, which has the largest flowers of any in the genus. Sprays of ornamental grasses, such as *Helictotrichon sempervirens*, 4 ft (1.2 m) high, *Stipa gigantea*, 6½ ft (2 m) high, and *Calamagrostis × acutiflora* 'Karl Foerster', 6 ft (1.8 m) high, all add extra pizzazz.

If you need to liven up a dull hedge or shrub, opt for the spectacularly colorful tropaeolums. Most of the tuberous kinds are "whip-through" climbers that sprint up taller plants, weaving in and out and flowering in vivid reds and yellows. The vigorous, rhizomatous climber *Tropaeolum speciosum* has vermilion flowers followed by bright blue berries. *T. ciliatum* is another spreader (considered a weed by some), with old-gold flowers veined red at the center. It can easily shoot 2.5 m (8 ft) in a season, and grows happily in the shade of a tree. Send it up the side of a house, or use it to decorate a fence. Both of these plants are frost hardy, and prefer a cool, moist site with slightly acid soil. *T. tuberosum* and its excellent cultivar var. *lineamaculatum* 'Ken Aslet' will be too tender for colder regions unless you give them a protective mulch over winter, or dig up the tubers and store them in a frostfree place and then replant in the following spring. The species is later flowering, while the cultivar gives a longer season. Beware of caterpillars.

In addition to the alliums described earlier, there are three smaller alliums grown for their exquisite, gentle flowers. *Allium beesianum* is 6 in (15 cm) high, has dangling white or blue star-shaped flowers and *A. oreophilum*, 8 in (20 cm) high, produces rich pink bell-shaped flowers. Grow both in a rock garden, where they can be viewed up close. *A. cernuum*, 16 in (40 cm) high, is one for the front of the border, with nodding, dark pink flowers.

If you need to liven up a dull hedge or shrub, opt for the spectacularly colorful tropaeolums, flowering in vivid reds and yellows.

Above: *Watsonia borbonica* is a half-hardy South African bulb that demands winter protection if it is to continue producing its colorful pink funnel-shaped flowers.

Far left and right: **If a border, needs jazzing up (far left), add a handful of gladioli corms.** *Gladiolus communis* subsp. *byzantinus* **will add a bright spark of color to a summer garden. It comes from the Mediterranean and, unlike the South African gladioli, is perfectly hardy. For a more dramatic effect, plant a block by itself (right), creating a big, bold clump of color. Don't worry about companion plants—this glamorous gladioli is striking enough to stand alone.**

If you are prepared to try your hand at some slightly trickier bulbs, the following three are well worth the effort. The half-hardy *Sparaxis tricolor*, 12 in (30 cm) high, produces colorful funnel-shaped flowers in orange and red, with bright central markings. It is best started into growth in a greenhouse for planting out in a dry summer. You can now buy special corms for spring planting outside; but in cool areas, treat them as annuals. Watsonias can also be started off in a frostfree greenhouse and then moved outside for the summer. They produce tall spires of gladiolus-type flowers. The half-hardy, purple-red *Watsonia fourcadei*, 3 ft (90 cm) high, is probably the one to try first, but snap up any kind you see, since they are highly attractive plants. Finally, try *Ixia viridiflora* for spring planting; in summer you will get thin spikes of gorgeous, white, star-shaped flowers, 12 in (30 cm) high, with striking, rich, purple-black centers. It is frost tender, so in cool areas treat it as an annual.

Irises

In summer, the spring irises give way to the tall bearded irises, ranging in height from 28 in to 4 ft (70 cm to 1.2 m). The color range is vast (they are available in all colors except pure red), the patterns highly intricate, and new developments mean that flower shapes are continually changing. As there is now such a wide selection available, a visit to a specialized nursery is recommended.

Scores of excellent cultivars have appeared over the past 25 years: these are stronger, better-formed, and offer a wider choice of color than the old irises. Look out for *Iris* 'Dusky Challenger', in deep blue-purple; *I.* 'Stratagem', in blue, red, pink and orange; or choose the old favorite *I.* 'Stepping Out', which is white with patterned, deep violet edges. The pink *I.* 'Saxon Princess' is remontant, meaning that it flowers again in the same year. Many irises have striking foliage: *I. pallida* 'Variegata', 4 ft (1.2 m) high, with its stiff, upright fan of green leaves with cream flashes along the edges, looks like a Mardi Gras headdress.

The bulbous blue-violet Spanish iris (*I. xiphium*), at 8–28 in (20–70 cm) high, thrives in sunny, well-drained soil, as do the related Dutch irises, which make good cut flowers— *I.* 'Bronze Queen' is an engaging mix of purple, bronze, and gold; and *I. latifolia* is a rich blue, violet or white. The miniature tall bearded irises, 16–26 in (40–65 cm) high, slip comfortably into a perennial border. One of the finest is *I.* 'Velvet Bouquet', which produces flowers in a lovely dark bluish-lilac shade.

The beardless rhizomatous Siberian irises are excellent, foolproof plants. They will thrive almost anywhere, although they prefer rich, moist, yet well-drained soil that does not get waterlogged in winter, and hate acid or alkaline soil. Plant them in shallow holes 2 in (5 cm) deep. The parent plant of many cultivars is the violet-blue *I. sibirica*, 32 in (80 cm) high, with attractive veining and white marking. Dozens of new cultivars are produced every year, with heights ranging from 2 to 4 ft (60 cm to 1.2 m); larger-flowered kinds are being developed, and colors include numerous shades of blue, violet, yellow, and pink. *I.* 'White Swirl' broke new ground in 1957 because it had horizontal, not pendent petals. The dashing *I.* 'Shirley Pope', 34 in (85 cm) high, has very dark red, almost black flowers with white patches. If you are looking for a spreader for dry or dampish

Numerous irises thrive in damp places, such as beside ponds, streams, or in moist beds.

shade, try *I. foetidissima*, 2 ft (60 cm) high, which is grown more for its fat, juicy-looking late autumn seeds than for its purplish summer flowers.

Numerous irises thrive in damp places, beside ponds and streams or in moist borders. The fully hardy, purple-red *Iris ensata*, 32 in (80 cm) high, is one of the great water-loving beauties. The Japanese were so moved by this iris that they created a ceremony dedicated to the opening of the flower. New, stronger, longer-lasting, more colorful cultivars are introduced regularly; they are known collectively as Japanese cultivars, and are about 3 ft (90 cm) in height. A fine example is *I. ensata* 'Sano-no-yuki'.

Iris ensata and its cultivars may be grown in containers with their rhizomes ½ in (1 cm) under water, but must be lifted to drier ground for the winter. The purple-blue *I. laevigata*, 32 in (80 cm) high, and the striking yellow *I. pseudacorus*, 4 ft (1.2 m) high, can both stand in water all year round, while *I. versicolor* 'Kermesina', claret-blue and 2 ft (60 cm) high, and *I. virginica*, lavender-blue and 34 in (85 cm) high, both prefer their roots in the bog garden and dislike being soaking wet all the time.

Far left: **The tall bearded** *Iris* **'Kent Pride' is a deep reddish-brown shade. It flowers in early summer. Close-up, these irises can look a little too fussy, but in a big group the overall effect is quite amazing.**

Left: **If you have boggy soil, try** *Iris laevigata*. **It grows wild in east Asian swamps, and tops its 16 in (40 cm) bladelike leaves with purple-blue flowers. The cultivar 'Variegata' is even better, its leaves patterned with pure white stripes.**

Below: *Iris pallida* **subsp.** *pallida* **forms a striking fan of erect, swordlike leaves, with silvery, papery bracts and soft-blue flowers.**

The exotics

For summer exotics—and I mean real show-stoppers—the cannas come top of the list. They produce showy leaves and flower spikes that can reach 8 ft (2.5 m). The question is, where to plant them? You could give them island beds in a lawn, but that is far too reminiscent of a municipal park, where they are lined up in immaculate rows. Far better to give them a subtropical border.

Canna musifolia produces bold, bananalike foliage and gains 8 ft (2.5 m) in height in a single summer. Grow it in a border with exotic shrubs and trees: standard daturas, with their highly scented, trumpet-shaped flowers; *Eucalyptus gunnii*, which produces gorgeous, new, blue rounded leaves; *Paulownia tomentosa*, whose large, pumped-up summer leaves flap like flags on a pole; and the spiky, giant yucca, *Yucca elephantipes*, which grows to 30 ft (10 m) high in the right climate. It is classified as tender, however, so must be kept warm over winter in a cooler climate. Add the vigorous, climbing blue *Solanum jasminoides* and the purple *Verbena bonariensis*, 5 ½ ft (1.7 m) high, and the cannas look just sensational.

There are currently about eighty cannas in total, with new cultivars constantly adding to the selection. In addition to *Canna musifolia*, try C. 'Wyoming', which reaches a lofty 6 ft (1.8 m),

and has bronze-purple foliage with an intense orange flower resembling a gladiolus topping it off. *C. indica*, reaching 6 ft (1.8 m), produces velvety bright red flowers, and C. 'Striata', 5 ft (1.5 m) high, has light green leaves with stylish yellow veining (crouch down and peer up at the light through the leaves). If the cannas are a little too flamboyant for your taste, try the dwarf cultivar C. 'Lucifer', which reaches just 2 ft (60 cm) high. If you have an ornamental pond, stand some cannas in the water, such as *C. glauca*, with its 16 in (40 cm) long leaves and pale yellow flowers. Cannas are half hardy, so in a frost-prone climate, lift the rhizomes when the stems blacken at the end of the season, and store them in cool, slightly damp leafmold or wood shavings. Pot them up the following spring for planting out in the yard later.

On a much smaller scale—about 12 in (30 cm) high—there is the sensational *Dichelostemma ida-maia*, the firecracker plant that grows on hillsides in Oregon and California. It has tubular

On a much smaller scale, there is the sensational *Dichelostemma ida-maia*, the firecracker plant.

Left: **The Californian firecracker,** *Dichelostemma ida-maia*, **is a fabulous, rarely seen flower. It needs first-rate drainage in bright sun to flower like this in early summer, and a good baking during its dormant stage.**

Right: **One of the best things about deep borders is that you can grow 8 ft (2.5 m) high cannas, with gaudy flowers and gigantic leaves. A touch of the tropics.**

guarantee the conditions, moving it outside to flower for eight weeks from mid-summer. *E. comosa*, with pinkish-white, star-shaped flowers, is becoming increasingly popular and will attract butterflies. The key to success with these bulbs is deep planting, at three times the depth of the bulb, in a free-draining, moist position, where they will not bake over summer. In winter, add a deep, protective mulch. If you are bringing them indoors, dry the bulbs in late autumn and keep them in a frostfree place until next spring. The fresh green foliage of *E. comosa* combines well with the deliciously scented chocolate-brown *Cosmos atrosanguineus* (beware of slugs) and dahlias.

Roscoea belong to the ginger family and come from high in the Himalayas. They have beautiful, distinguished orchidlike flowers, usually blue or purple, opening in succession. Remarkably hardy, they will withstand the coldest winters, but do need moist summer conditions, in gritty, free-draining soil, plenty of leafmold,

flowers in a startling bright red with greenish-white tips, produced in groups of eight per umbel. The tips gradually peel right back, turning yellowish and revealing a creamy interior. At the flowering stage, the leaves turn dull brown. Not easy to grow, they need sharply draining soil and a sunny position, where they can dry out after flowering. Firecrackers are frost hardy, but in areas where temperatures fall below 23°F (-5°C), they must be grown in pots in a greenhouse.

The pineapple flower, *Eucomis bicolor*, is a stylish and highly unusual plant from South Africa. At the base is a radiating array of horizontal leaves, with a vertical stem rising above, then a packed cylindrical batch of over 100 tiny, lime-green, hyacinth-like flowers, crowned with a tuft of pineapplelike green leaves. The whole plant is approximately 18 in (45 cm) high. The genus name is Greek, meaning beautiful hair ("eu" meaning good, and "kome" hair). It is of borderline hardiness (fully to frost hardy), so is probably best grown in a pot in cooler climates, where you can and dry winters. If the latter is hard to provide, they can be kept under cover in pots. Look out for *Roscoea cautleyoides*, 18 in (45 cm) high, in pale yellow, white, or purple; *R. scillifolia* and *R. purpurea* are both purple and 12 in (30 cm) high, the latter flowering into autumn.

The Mexican *Tigridia pavonia*, 20 in (50 cm) high, has exquisite irislike flowers, usually in bright red, with a red- and white-mottled center. There are plenty of cultivars available in different colors. The flowers are short-lived—lasting only one day—but they appear in rapid succession. Growing them is not a problem, but they dislike frosts, so in cool climates start them off in a greenhouse and bring them indoors in autumn.

Zantedeschia aethiopica, an extremely beautiful exotic for a bog garden, has a reputation for being slightly tender, but if planted at least 6 in (15 cm) deep, it should survive winter frosts. It even grows in water when planted up to 12 in (30 cm) deep. It is well worth taking the risk, because from mid-summer to early autumn it unfurls terrific white funnel-shaped spathes, held well above bold, glossy arrow-shaped leaves, reaching 3 ft (90 cm) high, followed by yellow berries. If you live in a cold region, *Z. aethiopica* 'Crowborough' is said to be the hardiest cultivar.

Finally, adored by children, is the toad lily (*Tricyrtis formosana*). This is a fabulous, if bizarre, little rhizomatous plant that resembles a fat, hunched creature, with shiny, star-shaped, white to mauve-pink flowers and crimson spots. It likes dappled shade and fertile, moist, well-drained soil. While it generally flowers in autumn, it can start opening in a hot, late summer.

Far left: **In late summer, the Giant pineapple flower,** *Eucomis pallidiflora*, **sends up long spikes packed with greenish-white flowers, with a small tuft of leaves on the top. The bulbs need hunting out, but are well worth a try.**

Left: *Roscoea cautleyoides* **has curious orchidlike flowers and silky petals like** crumpled tissue paper. **Roscoeas are not strictly bulbs, but have small rhizomes and tuberous roots. They like to be moist in summer and dry in winter.**

Right: **The poised white flowers of** *Zantedeschia aethiopica* **'Crowborough' hover elegantly above the glossy, broad green leaves.**

Scented bulbs

The scented lilies are undoubtedly the most glorious of all the fragrant summer bulbs. Less experienced gardeners are often reluctant to try lilies: they assume that because they are exotic-looking, they will be fussy, impossible plants to grow. While this is the case with some, many lilies could not be easier to cultivate.

The greatest threat to lilies is the slug. There is nothing crueler, more rage-filling, than watching a lily stem shoot up, worshipping the fattening buds, than coming out one morning to find the stem snapped at right angles, completely eaten through. As a result, they are best grown in pots to provide some protection, or use various methods of control (*see page* 77).

The three key essentials for growing lilies are shading the base with other plants, providing plenty of sun for the top growth, and soil with good drainage. Lily bulbs obtained in the fall should be planted straight away. In frost-prone areas, keep them in pots in a cool room, watering occasionally, for planting out next spring. If your soil or climate is not suitable, grow lilies in pots and cluster them with other containers, or stand them in

If you are feeling mischievous, try the tuberous *Dracunculus vulgaris*, 3 ft (90 cm) high.

beds of roses. In the perennial border, let them flower above the steely blue-tinged *Eryngium giganteum*, 30 in (75 cm) high, or the white *Lychnis coronaria* Alba Group, 32 in (80 cm). Give lilies special beds, or stand the pots under an arbor where you can snooze in the summer savoring their sweet fragrance.

The most fail-safe of all the lilies is *Lilium regale*. These richly scented white bulbs grow about 4½ ft (1.4 m) high, and deserve center stage when flowering. There are scores of other perfumed lilies. The species include the spectacular but short-lived *L. auratum*, 4 ft (1.2 m) high, with white, yellow-streaked flowers; *L. duchartrei*, 3 ft (90 cm) high, which is white marbled with purple spots; and *L. hansonii*, 3–5 ft (90 cm–1.5 m), with deep orange-yellow waxy flowers. Attractive hybrids include *L.* 'Casa Blanca', which is pure white, and *L.* 'Journey's End', crimson-pink in color, both reaching 4 ft (1.2 m) high. The cut-flower trade, especially in America, is continually producing new plants. One of the most prodigious recent lilies is *L.* 'Black Beauty'. Not only does it produce up to 150 flowers per stem, but it is dark crimson, almost black, in color, grows 5 ft (1.5 m) high, multiplies freely, and is almost indestructible.

Cardiocrinum giganteum, the giant lily that originates in forests in the Himalayas, is a vast, spectacular summer bulb. In the right conditions, the flower spikes can reach a magnificent 6½ ft (2 m), with white trumpet flowers emitting a gentle scent. It needs a cool, moist, woodland-type area of the garden, and likes partial shade and rich soil. Although it is fully hardy, new growth does need frost protection (use a pile of bracken). The giant lily is monocarpic and dies after flowering, but offsets develop each year, each needing three to four years to mature. Do not attempt to grow it from seed—it can take eight years.

Hedychium gardnerianum, from Nepal and Assam, India, is the best of the ginger lilies, with a stem height of 6½ ft (2 m), and spikes of deliciously fragrant, lemon-yellow flowers. They are

Far left: *Lilium* 'Casa Blanca' exudes a delicious scent in summer. Never stint on lilies—they look like prima donnas, demanding kid-glove treatment, but are mainly hardy. The key requirements are flowers in sun with the stem base in shade, and summer moisture combined with good drainage.

Right: **Slugs love lilies, and one of the best ways to ward off attacks is by growing the bulbs in pots.**

Below: **The wonderfully weird** *Dracunculus vulgaris* **emits a less than delightful smell.**

frost-tender, although they can survive temperatures as low as 25° F (-7° C) for short periods. In frost-prone climates, keep them in a sunroom until the summer, when they may be planted outdoors in a subtropical bed. If you get hooked on these, there are about forty other kinds of ginger lilies to try. For a deep, rich orange hue, try the 6½ ft (2 m) high *H. coccineum* 'Tara'.

If you are feeling mischievous, try the dramatic tuberous *Dracunculus vulgaris*, 3 ft (90 cm) high. It looks quite sinister, with its blotchy, snakelike stem and a velvety maroon-purple spathe that smells of rotting meat, attracting pollinating flies. However, it is popular, has attractive divided foliage, and is easily grown, provided it has frost protection.

SUMMER GALLERY

Allium (Onion)

Height: 2½ in– 6½ ft (6 cm–2 m), spread: 2–8 in (5–20 cm); flowers in midsummer; mostly fully hardy

A large group of some 700 species, mainly bulbous perennials, producing architectural drumsticklike white, mauve, blue, or yellow flowers. Many have foliage that smells of onions when crushed. Prefer fertile, well-drained soil in full sun. Excellent for drying and cut flowers.

Alstroemeria (Peruvian lily)

Height: 6–36 in (15–90 cm), spread: 6–36 in (15–90 cm); flowers in summer; mostly fully hardy

Showy tuberous or rhizomatous perennials with flowers in a wide color range. Need moist, fertile, well-drained soil and a bright position. Dislike excessive dryness.

Canna (Indian shot plant)

Height: 2–8 ft (60 cm–2.5 m), spread: 20–24 in (50–60 cm); flowers in midsummer to early fall; half hardy

Generally large, exotic-looking rhizomatous perennials in a range of colors from scarlet-orange to pink and white. Require fertile soil and bright sun. Dislike excessive dryness.

Cardiocrinum giganteum (Giant lily)

Height: 6½ ft (2 m), spread: 18 in (45 cm); flowers in mid- to late summer; fully hardy

Stunning bulbous perennial bearing tall spires covered with enormous lilylike, trumpet-shaped scented white flowers. Requires moist, humus-rich, shady, well-drained soil. Dislikes excessive dryness.

Crocosmia (Montbretia)

Height: 16–36 in (40–90 cm), spread 3–4 in (8–10 cm); mid- to late summer; mostly fully hardy

Cormous perennials bearing sprays of brightly colored funnel-shaped flowers in fiery hues, especially scarlet, red, orange, and yellow, among swordlike leaves. Require full sun or dappled shade, in moist, well-drained soil. Dislike excessive dryness and disturbance. Provide a protective mulch in cold winters. The orange Crocosmia masoniorum makes a useful cut flower.

Dierama pulcherrimum (Angel's fishing rod, wandflower)

Height: 4 ft (1.2 m), spread: 2 ft (60 cm); flowers in late summer to early autumn; mature clumps fully hardy

Graceful cormous perennial with slender arching stems bearing bell-shaped, magenta-pink to purple-red flowers. Requires fertile, moist but well-drained soil in full sun. Beware of waterlogging. Does not transplant well. Freely seeds and spreads.

Gladiolus hybrids and cultivars

Height: 5½ ft (1.7 m), spread 2–6 in (5–15 cm); flowers early to late summer; half hardy

Elegant cormous perennials with a wide color range including bright reds, yellows, and pinks. Fussy plants—they require a bed of sharp sand, on fertile soil, in a sheltered, sunny site, and staking. Apply fungicide before planting. Give a high-potash tomato feed in growth, and water regularly when dry. Lift in winter, remove the new cormlets, and store in frost-free conditions, then plant out in late spring. Excellent cut flowers.

Iris pseudacorus (Yellow flag)

Height: 4 ft (1.2 m), spread: 12–18 in (30–45 cm); flowers in mid- and late summer; fully hardy

Water-loving rhizomatous perennial with striking clear yellow flowers and lush blue-green strap-shaped spears of foliage. Can stand in shallow water all year or grow in a moist, boggy bed. May be invasive. Iris pseudacorus 'Variegata' is less invasive and bolder, with yellow-white stripes on the leaves that fade to green after midsummer.

Kniphofia (Red-hot poker, torch lily)

Height: 1–6 ft (30 cm–1.8 m), spread 10–30 in (25–75 cm) ; flowers in late summer to early autumn; mostly fully hardy

Architectural, rhizomatous perennials with mostly brightly colored, red and yellow distinctive bottlebrush-shaped flowers rising above a thick clump of narrow grasslike or strap-shaped leaves. Require a hot, sunny position on quick-draining, sandy soil. In a perennial bed, makes for a lively mix with other spike- and spire-shaped plants.

Lilium duchartrei (Lily)

Height: 3 ft (90 cm), spread: 6–12 in (15–30 cm); flowers in midsummer; fully hardy

Strikingly beautiful bulbous perennial with maroon-marbled white flowers in a Turk's-cap shape. Prefers fertile soil in bright sun or dappled shade.

Lilium hansonii (Lily)

Height: 3–5 ft (1–1.5 m), spread: 6–10 in (15–25 cm); flowers in early summer; fully hardy

Fragrant bulbous perennial with orange-yellow, waxy blooms with purple-brown spots; the thick petals are tightly recurved or tightly pulled back in a Turk's-cap shape. Grow in moist but well-drained soil, with plenty of added leafmold, in dappled shade, with shade at the base.

Lilium regale (Regal lily)

Height: 4 ½ ft (1.4 m), spread: 6–8 in (15–20 cm); flowers in midsummer; fully hardy

Scented bulbous perennial with richly fragrant, white trumpet-shaped flowers that have purple veining on the outside, and a yellow throat and golden anthers inside. Prefers fertile, well-drained soil, with flowers in full sun and bases in the shade. Excellent planted in pots and for cutting.

Lilium Pink Perfection Group (Lily)

Height: 5 ft (1.5 m), spread: 10–12 in (25–30 cm); flowers in midsummer; fully hardy

Perfumed bulbous perennials with generally deep pink or dark purple-red, nodding, trumpet-shaped flowers, with up to 36 blooms on each stout stem. Grow in fertile soil, in bright sun, with shade at the bases. Strongly and deliciously scented.

Nectaroscordum siculum subsp. bulgaricum

Height: 3 ft (90 cm), spread: 4 in (10 cm); flowers in early summer; fully hardy

Bulbous perennial related to the Allium family, with creamy white, nodding bell-shaped flowers, tinged red and green. Requires light, fertile, well-drained ground in bright sun. Can be invasive. Excellent for dried winter arrangements.

Tricyrtis formosana (Toad lily)

Height: 30 in (75 cm), spread: 18 in (45 cm); flowers in late summer or autumn; fully hardy

Unusual rhizomatous perennial with star-shaped flowers in white to bright pink patterned with crimson. Requires humus-rich, moist, well-drained soil in light shade.

Tropaeolum tuberosum var. lineamaculatum 'Ken Aslet'

Height: 8½ ft (2.5 m); flowers in midsummer; half hardy

Orange-flowered, tuberous perennial climber requiring moist but well-drained soil in a bright place. Half-hardy, the tuber must be lifted in the fall and kept in a frost-free place for replanting the next spring.

Zantedeschia aethiopica (Arum lily)

Height: 3 ft (90 cm), spread: 2 ft (60 cm); flowers from late spring to midsummer; frost hardy

Water-loving rhizomatous perennials with white spathes and yellow spadices. Requires fertile, moist soil, in full sun or light shade. Suitable for bogs and water margins.

Right: *Lilium regale*

We are all familiar with spring and summer bulbs, but few realize that there are also some absolute crackers for the fall. Many are punchy and vivid, providing a glorious splash of bold color before autumn bows out, giving way to the cooler, more somber shades of winter.

AUTUMN

Dahlias

Where autumn color is needed, dahlias are an absolute must. They start flowering in midsummer, but keep going through the fall: wonderful blobs of color emerging through the mists like traffic lights, until they are blackened by frost.

Dahlias originated in Central and South America, and did not reach Europe until the late 18th century. There are now approximately 20 thousand cultivars, botanically divided into ten groups, according to the shape of their flowerheads. One of the most striking groups are the cactus-flowered dahlias, with rounded, spiky flowerheads, 4–6 in (10–15 cm) across, or the pompon group, with amazingly spherical flowerheads up to 2 in (5 cm) wide. Colors include yellow, orange, red, and pink. Dahlias are not for growing in subtle, understated arrangements: they should shriek dramatically across the garden, so plant them *en masse* in large, concentrated blocks. Heights vary, but there are plenty in the 3–4½ ft (90 cm–1.3 m) range.

One of the most well-known dahlias is the velvety scarlet *Dahlia* 'Bishop of Llandaff', 3 ft (90 cm) high, with rich, dark foliage. In Monet's garden in Giverny it is combined, in huge, magnificent dahlia arrangements, with *D.* 'Aumonier Chandelon', with red flowers; *D.* 'Hayley Jayne', with purple-pink and white semicactus blooms; and *D.* 'Jescot Julie', with orchid-shaped flowers in orange-red. Dahlias are made for hothouse borders, combined with cormous crocosmias, rhizomatous cannas, and kaffir lilies (*Schizostylis coccinea*). Excellent neighboring non-bulbs include the red-flowering cultivars of the tobacco plant *Nicotiana* × *sanderae*, 12 in (30 cm) high, *Penstemon* 'Rubicundus', 30 in (75 cm) high, and the 'Ruffles' zinnias, 2 ft (60 cm) high, which look like pompon dahlias at a distance. For contrast, grow dahlias against a spiky-leaved, smoky brown *Cordyline australis* and the scarlet sage *Salvia fulgens*, 3 ft (90 cm) high. Bright yellow *Helianthus* and white *Bracteantha bracteata* 'King Size Silvery White' also make good planting partners. Dahlias are quite convivial.

Dahlias require plenty of care for best results: if you perform, they will perform. Grow them in fertile, well-drained soil, with plenty of well-rotted manure, in full sun. Tubers showing leaves cannot be planted until after the last frost; the leafless can

Dahlias combine extremely well in hothouse borders with cormous crocosmias, rhizomatous cannas, and kaffir lilies (*Schizostylis coccinea*).

withstand the final cold snap. Water growing plants well and provide a nitrogen feed until the buds form, then switch to a tomato fertilizer. Pinch out the growing tips four weeks after planting to encourage branching, and stake the taller cultivars. Check regularly for slugs and earwigs.

In mild areas, leave the dahlias in the ground over winter. In colder climates, lift the tubers in winter when the leaves start to blacken at the ends, clean off the mud, and after about ten days, cut away the stem to 4 in (10 cm). Dry the tubers, then trim away any straggly roots, and dust with yellow sulfur. Store them in boxes filled with sand and keep them at a constant, cool but frostfree temperature. Plant up the following spring, dividing each tuber into two or three pieces, each one with a bud. It may sound time-consuming, but dahlias are well worth the effort.

Far left, left and above: **Dahlias originate from Central and South America. It's thought that they were once used as an animal crop by the Aztecs as well as a human medicine. And today? They provide an indispensible blast of border color from midsummer right through to fall frosts. If you have only room for one, try the 'Bishop of Llandaff' (far left). The bronze-red foliage is topped by a mass of intense scarlet semidouble flowers. Other favorite dahlias include 'Fascination', a classic waterlily dahlia (left), which is in complete contrast to the perfectly spherical form of the miniature pompon 'Kathryn's Cupid' (above).**

Colchicums

Often known as autumn crocuses, colchicums are not, in fact, in any way related to true crocuses. Marked differences are that colchicums have six stamens while crocuses have only three, and the pink of colchicums is richer than that of crocuses. Their other common name, naked ladies, refers to the absence of leaves at flowering time in autumn; these don't open until the spring.

Among the best of the colchicums is *Colchicum autumnale*, 5 in (13 cm) high, which produces a cluster of soft pink, long-tubed goblet-shaped flowers that look wonderfully starry when open. There is also a lovely white form *C. a.* 'Album'; as well as a double white, *C. a.* 'Alboplenum'; and a double pink *C. a.* 'Pleniflorum'. The best purple is probably the tiny *C. atropurpureum*, at 2 in (5 cm) high, but for more impact try the taller *C. speciosum*, with its larger, deep purple-pink flowers with a white throat, at 6 in (15 cm) high. It looks good beside the

red, poisonous autumn berries of the 10 in (25 cm) high *Arum italicum* 'Marmoratum', or *Iris foetidissima*, 18 in (45 cm) high, with its cheerful orange autumn–winter seed pods. The white form, *Colchicum speciosum* 'Album', is also well worth trying.

You can certainly grow colchicums in grass—*Colchicum speciosum* is a particularly good naturalizer, creating a striking display—but unlike true crocuses, they do not always increase well. A much better bet is to grow them in a perennial bed, popping through *Artemisia schmidtiana*, which forms a low, 12-in (30-cm) high silver-gray cover, or fronting a strong red hedge of *Fuchsia* 'Riccartonii', which can grow to 8 ft (2.4 m).

Left: **The white *Colchicum speciosum* 'Album' have an elegant fragility. They naturalize easily and look wonderful planted in rough grass, their large goblet-shaped flowers surrounded by a carpet of green.**

Above: ***Colchicum speciosum* is the best colchicum for a fall display. The flowers are large and sturdy, excellent at withstanding heavy rain or high winds. Note that the flowers appear in autumn, the foliage appears in spring.**

Crocuses

The true autumn-flowering crocuses provide a brief, sharp burst of color. At less than 6 in (15 cm) high, they are excellent plants for pepping up the garden. Plant them in large groups in a warm, sunny site, which will encourage the flowers to open out fully.

Interesting also is the rich purple-blue *Crocus sativus*, from which the spice saffron is obtained.

The first to flower in early autumn is the lilac *Crocus kotschyanus*, 4 in (10 cm) high, which multiplies freely. The scented *C. longiflorus* is a little more gaudy, with lilac petals and yellow anthers, whose flowers appear with the leaves. The purple *C. nudiflorus* is the best crocus for naturalizing in grass, thriving in heavy, moist meadows and partial shade. The delightful lilac-blue *C. speciosus* or its forms like *C. s.* 'Albus', in white, or *C. s.* 'Aitchisonii' in pale lilac, are also good garden plants. *C. banaticus* is a wonderful little curiosity: its lavender flowers resemble those of an iris, with the three outer segments larger than the inner three. Interesting also is the rich purple-blue *C. sativus*, from which the spice saffron is obtained. Saffron crocuses need a warm, dry summer dormancy in well-drained soil, and deep planting at 6 in (15 cm). Of all the autumn-flowering crocuses, the pick of the bunch is probably the scented *C. goulimyi*, with a long, slender perianth tube, and gobletlike flowers in lilac, or its cultivar *C. g.* 'Mani White'.

Left: **The soft violet-blue *Crocus speciosus* is an easy-to-grow autumn crocus. As with spring crocuses, plant** **this autumn variety in huge, sweeping groups. It is an excellent naturalizer, and will spread freely through grass.**

Snowdrops, snowflakes, and autumn daffodils

Most snowdrops appear in the spring, but there is also an autumn kind, *Galanthus reginae-olgae*, 4 in (10 cm) high, which sometimes lasts into midwinter. It differs only slightly from the spring snowdrops: the leaves are a dull deep green, with a central pale gray line. It also requires a brighter, sunnier, warmer position than most snowdrops. The flowers open before the leaves.

The moisture-loving spring snowflakes (*Leucojum*) have two delicate autumn-flowering white relatives, both 6 in (15 cm) high: *Leucojum autumnale*, found in woodlands and stony grassland; and *L. valentinum*, originating in bright, stony outcrops. The former likes a dry summer, so that the bulbs can bake; the latter has larger flowers and is slightly more tender, needing shelter at the foot of a wall.

For a sunny rock garden the bright yellow sternbergias, commonly known as autumn daffodils, are an excellent choice. Despite their name, they are not actually related to daffodils—they look more like large yellow crocuses—nor do they all flower in the fall. *Sternbergia lutea*, with its goblet-shaped flowers reaching 12 in (30 cm) in height, and *S. sicula*, at a quarter of the size and with star-shaped flowers, are the ones to choose for the autumn months. Plant the bulbs in a hot spot, where they can bake over summer, and where the yellow of the flowers gets picked up by the sun. If you are visiting the Mediterranean, look for *Sternbergia lutea* growing wild around olive trees.

Left: **The most commonly available autumn snowdrop is** *Galanthus reginae-olgae*. **It thrives particularly well in a bright and sunny corner of a rock garden, where it can dry out during the summer.**

Above: **The yellow-flowering** *Sternbergia lutea* **is a terrific little Mediterranean bulb. Grow at the front of the border, in rock gardens, or in gravel. Hot sun and good drainage is essential.**

Cyclamen

The free-flowering, self-seeding pink *Cyclamen hederifolium*, 10 cm (4 in) tall, is excellent for naturalizing. Originating in the Mediterranean, it is extremely hardy and will happily tolerate light shade. The low-growing, charming flowers are small and graceful, with silky swept-back petals. On slender stems, they hover above the attractive cyclamen leaves, which are glorious from fall right through winter to spring, come in a great variety of shapes, and are almost ivylike, with patterned silvery markings on a green background. The markings on *C. h.* Bowles' Apollo Group are possibly the best of all.

The dry, often neglected ground under a tree is the best place for *C. hederifolium*. Brown, bare patches of soil will soon be covered in a densely clustered carpet of pink, or white in the case of *C. h.* f. *album*. The tubers themselves defy belief. They look like wizened, wrinkly, corklike, flattened disks, with all the zest of an old chunk of gingerroot, but can let loose scores of flowers. These cyclamen need a well-drained site and an annual leafmold mulch, particularly in shadier areas.

Cyclamen leaves, which are glorious from autumn through winter to spring, come in a great variety of shapes, and are ivylike, with patterned silvery markings.

Right: *Cyclamen hederifolium* is the earliest-flowering and most colorful cyclamen. It is ideal for ideal for planting in clumps around trees, as it is happy growing in a cool spot in dappled shade. The twin benefits are pink flowers followed by gorgeous, silver and green marbled foliage.

Warm border companions

If you want a genuine autumn gladiolus, then the South African *Gladiolus papilio*, 3 ft (90 cm) high, is quite exquisite. It has open, bell-shaped flowers in faded purple, green, and cream, and spreads freely. The corms are fairly tender, but if planted in the spring after the last frost, they should survive the following winter outside, provided they have a protective covering of bracken when the temperature drops. The showy *Crinum × powellii* makes a good companion: a fellow South African bulb, 4 ft (1.2 m) high, which has lily-scented, trumpet-shaped, rose-pink flowers (white in *C. × p.* 'Album'). The only drawback is the foliage, which can become scruffy. *C. × powellii* and its cultivars need a warm, sunny site in fertile, well-drained soil, and regular watering. In frost-prone regions, plant with the neck of the bulb at soil level, and give it a protective winter mulch.

Another outstanding gladiolus is the simple but highly ornamental, sweetly scented *Gladiolus callianthus* 'Murieliae'. This is one of those rare plants that takes your breath away. It has pure white open flowers, standing 3 ft (90 cm) clear of the ground, with a beautiful rich purple throat. If it has not flowered before the first frosts, bring it indoors in a pot to open. A frost-tender bulb, it needs lifting over winter in frost-prone areas, and repotting again the following spring.

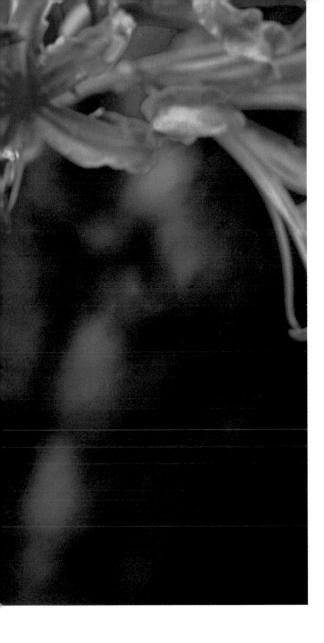

Above: **Just when you think the autumn border is past its best, the wonderfully decorative South African nerines put in an appearance.** *Nerine bowdenii* **is the hardiest species, and has startling, bright pink flowers with elegantly ruffled, reflexed petals carried on slender stems that reach nearly 28 in (70 cm) in height.**

Above right: **Don't be put off by the sometimes rather scruffy foliage of** *Crinum × powellii.* **It has nicely scented, showy rose-pink trumpet-shaped flowers.**

Right: *Gladiolus callianthus* 'Murieliae' has beautiful, starry, white flowers, as well as a sweet scent that is most evident in the evenings.

The third ingredient for a warm South African-type bed is the stout *Nerine bowdenii*, the hardiest nerine and the one to leave out all year, especially against a sunny wall. Plant it with the neck of the bulb just showing above the soil. It has umbels of up to nine light pink flowers, like tiny lilies with ruffled margins, and reaches 28 in (70 cm) in height. Cultivars include *N. b.* 'Mark Fenwick', which is more vigorous and grows slightly taller, producing darker pink flowers; *N. b.* 'Pink Triumph', another deep pink cultivar, which is shorter, at 18 in (45 cm); and the reddish-pink *N. bowdenii* 'Lady Llewellyn'.

For end-of-season zing, the stunning and exotic kaffir lilies (*Schizostylis coccinea*), also from South Africa, are very hard to beat. Their gladioluslike flowers, 2 ft (60 cm) high, come in several delicious colors: *Schizostylis coccinea* 'Jennifer' has superb clear pink flowers; *S. c.* 'Major' has large red bloom with a rich silky sheen; *S. c.* 'Sunrise' is salmon-pink; and

S. c. 'Viscountess Byng' bears flowers in a pretty pale pink. Their narrow leaves are strap shaped and fresh green, a welcome sight at a time when the foliage of other plants around them are turning. Kaffir lilies ideally like a damp area beside water, but will also grow happily in a moist bed.

The third ingredient for a warm South African-type bed is the stout *Nerine bowdenii*, the hardiest nerine.

Foliage plants and ornamental grasses will provide added visual interest to a mixed border and act as a background to autumn bulbs. The evergreen rue, *Ruta graveolens* 'Jackman's Blue', 2 ft (60 cm) high, provides a neat, dense build-up of blue-tinged foliage, and the arching plume-topped grass *Hordeum jubatum*, 18 in (45 cm) high, with its silky heads, provides a soft, swirling background without being too dominant. A taller grass alternative is *Pennisetum villosum*, 2 ft (60 cm) high, with fluffy, feathery white plumes waving above a thick clump of gray-green leaves. It can succumb to frost, so plant it in a container and bring it indoors over winter. Another excellent perennial-bed plant for the fall is the clump-forming perennial *Gaura lindheimeri*, which is covered with clusters of small flowers on long wiry stems. It starts flowering in late spring and keeps going all through the summer right up until early autumn. It grows 30 in (75 cm) high.

Far left: **The lipstick-pink South African rhizome** *Schizostylis coccinea* **'Major' loves damp and boggy areas, but will also happily grow in a bed. However, don't let it dry out in summer.**

Left: **This informal autumn border is a riot of different colors and shapes, crammed with a mass of nerines, asters, dianthus, artemisia, and the self-seeding, purple** *Verbena bonariensis*.

AUTUMN GALLERY

Colchicum autumnale (Meadow saffron)

Height: 5 in (13 cm), spread: 3 in (8 cm); flowers in mid- to late autumn; fully hardy

Vigorous cormous perennial with goblet-like, rosy pink to white flowers. Requires fertile, well-drained soil in full sun. Flowers before the foliage, which appears in spring.

Crinum × powellii

Height: 4 ft (1.2 m), spread: 12 in (30 cm); flowers in late summer to autumn; borderline fully hardy

Scented bulbous perennial with trumpet-shaped pink flowers. Plant in a warm, sunny site in moist, humus-rich, well-drained soil and leave undisturbed. Grow in pots in shallow water in summer.

Crocus goulimyi

Height: 4 in (10 cm), spread: 2 in (5 cm); flowers in early to mid-autumn; fully hardy

Cormous perennial producing lilac flowers with distinctive long tubes. Thrives in moderately fertile soil in a sunny, sheltered position. Increases freely.

Cyclamen hederifolium

Height: 4 in (10 cm), spread: 6 in (15 cm); flowers in mid- and late autumn; fully hardy

Tuberous perennial with pink flowers and green, silvery mottled foliage. Requires fertile, well-drained soil in sun or dappled shade, and leafmold. Likes dry summers; a place under trees is ideal.

Dahlia 'Bishop of Llandaff'

Height: 3 ft (90 cm), spread: 18 in (45 cm); flowers in midsummer to autumn; frost tender

Striking tuberous perennial bearing velvety red flowers above dark copper-red foliage. Needs fertile, well-drained soil in full sun, and plenty of well-rotted manure.

Galanthus reginae-olgae (Snowdrop)

Height: 4 in (10 cm), spread: 2 in (5 cm); flowers in autumn, sometimes to midwinter; frost hardy

Delicate bulbous perennial with duller green foliage than other snowdrops. Grow in well-drained soil that does not dry out in summer, in a sheltered spot in bright dappled shade.

Gladiolus callianthus 'Murieliae'

Height: 3 ft (90 cm), spread: 2 in (5 cm); flowers in late summer and early autumn; frost tender

Sweetly scented cormous perennial with white open flowers with a beautiful purple neck. Plant at the foot of a sunny wall in well-drained soil, or grow in a sunroom.

Gladiolus papilio

Height: 3 ft (90 cm), spread: 3 in (8 cm); flowers in late summer to autumn; frost to fully hardy

Graceful cormous perennial in intriguing color combinations: faded purple, green, and cream. Requires fertile, well-drained soil in bright sun. In cold areas, grow in pots in a sunroom, or mulch deeply in winter.

Leucojum autumnale (Snowflake)

Height: 6 in (15 cm), spread: 2 in (5 cm); flowers in late summer and early autumn; fully hardy

Slender bulbous perennial with nodding, white bell-shaped flowers. Thrives in well-drained soil in bright sun, particularly in summer, but tolerates shade at other times.

Nerine bowdenii

Height: 28 in (70 cm), spread: 3 in (8 cm); flowers in early to mid-autumn; fully hardy

Strong-stemmed bulbous perennial with bright pink flowers and strap-shaped leaves. Requires shallow planting in well-drained soil at the foot of a hot, sunny wall.

Schizostylis coccinea (Kaffir lily)

Height: 2 ft (60 cm), spread: 12 in (30 cm); flowers from late summer to early winter; frost hardy

Vigorous rhizomatous perennial with scarlet flowers and long, thin, strap-shaped leaves. Thrives in moist, well-drained soil in bright sun, near water or in a perennial bed.

Sternbergia lutea (Autumn daffodil)

Height: 30 cm (12in), spread: 5 cm (2 in); flowers mid-autumn; frost hardy

Free-flowering bulbous perennial with a daffodillike bulb producing rich yellow flowers. Grow at the foot of a sunny wall, in well-drained soil. Needs a dry summer baking and a protective winter mulch.

Above: *Colchicum autumnale* 'Album'

Above right: *Crocus goullamyl*

Right: *Schizostylis coccinea* 'Sunrise'

Far right: *Cyclamen hederifolium*

Below left: *Dahlia* 'Bishop of Llandaff'

Below far right: *Sternbergia lutea*

Opposite page: *Dahlia* 'Glorie van Heemstede'

After the glories of autumn, winter can seem bleak by comparison. However, gardeners need not despair. The garden may be dominated by the gray-browns of bark, bare soil, twigs, and catkins, but there are flashes of color from evergreens and berries, as well as a good selection of winter bulbs.

WINTER

Colorful displays

More than at any other time, the basic framework of the garden is on display in winter—you have an X-ray view, with the bones of woody plants exposed. At this time of year, winter-flowering bulbs have an important role to play: planted between shrubs and trees or in pots, they bring splashes of much-needed color and cheer.

The big star of the winter garden is the pale pink, magenta, or white *Cyclamen coum*. Grow it among the autumn-flowering *Cyclamen hederifolium*, naturalized in grass or in borders. The flowers of *C. coum* look magnificent set against the silver-mottled foliage of *C. hederifolium*, and the two combined will guarantee a long display from autumn through to winter. Both cyclamens thrive in well-drained soil with plenty of leafmold, and dappled shade. *C. coum* can be slightly tricky, but persevere, as it is an excellent garden plant. There are also plenty of forms to try: *C. c.* f. *albissimum*, in white with magenta markings at the base of the kidney-shaped petals; *C. c.* 'Meaden's Crimson', with deep, rich crimson flowers; and the wonderful *C. c.* f. *coum* 'Tilebarn Elizabeth', which is dark and pale pink. Combine them with *C. c.* f. *c.* 'Silver Star' whose silvery leaves catch the sun.

Like the cyclamens, the winter crocuses guarantee swathes of color, given the right conditions. The lilac *Crocus laevigatus* 'Fontenayi', 3 in (8 cm) high, is a late autumn to midwinter flowerer, with lilac-purple flowers and purple feathered markings on the outside of the petals. Equally good, and with plenty of color choice from its hybrids and cultivars, is *C. chrysanthus*. It is an easy spreader and will vigorously make a blanket of cream or yellow across grassy banks or lawns. There are about 35 forms, including *C. c.* 'Romance', with its yellow flowers with gray-blue markings on the outer petals; *C. c.* 'Ladykiller', which has bold bluish-purple flowers with a white interior; and *C. c.* 'Gipsy Girl',

Far left and below: **Don't think crocuses are exclusively for spring, they flower in winter too.** The cultivars of *Crocus chrysanthus* appear in the New Year in a good range of colors. 'Ladykiller' (far left) is violet outside and white within, while 'Cream Beauty' (below) lives up to its name. Plant crocuses in a sunny spot with good drainage— a rock garden is ideal.

Left: *Cyclamen coum* f. *albissimum*. Though this cyclamen is scentless, unlike the florists' tender *Cyclamen persicum*, it is a totally invaluable plant for the winter garden. It is a hardy, colorful spreader with attractive foliage markings. There are several excellent *coum* cultivars, the Pewter group perhaps offering the best silvery foliage effects.

Like the cyclamens, the winter crocuses guarantee swathes of color, given the right conditions.

a creamy yellow-flowered cultivar with feathered purple markings patterning the outside. Another vigorous crocus with the added benefit of delicate but delicious scent is *Crocus sieberi* 'Hubert Edelstein' in pale lilac with rich purple markings.

Irises

Most irises flower from spring to summer, but there are several kinds that bloom over winter, even in cold, frost-prone regions. *Iris unguicularis*, 12 in (30 cm) high, is a reliable winter-to-spring flowerer with scented lilac flowers. It prefers extremely poor, stony limestone soil at the foot of a sunny wall, but will tolerate more fertile ground; just keep slugs at bay. *I. u.* 'Alba' is creamy white, and *I. u.* 'Mary Barnard' deep violet.

For small, front-of-the-bed or rock garden irises, try *Iris reticulata*, which is violet-blue with yellow markings, or some of the Reticulata Hybrids, such as *I.* 'J. S. Dijt', with gently scented, reddish-purple flowers with orange marks; *I.* 'Cantab', whose flowers have bold yellow marks against pale blue; or the new *I.* 'George' with its large flowers in rich purple with yellow marks edged white. *I. danfordiae,* with its solitary yellow flower with greenish-yellow markings, is another Reticulata Hybrid. However, it will not flower year after year, since the bulb divides after flowering into smaller bulbils, which take years to reach flowering size. Treat it as an annual, starting afresh each year.

One of the best winter irises is *Iris histrioides*, which appears mid-season, and robustly survives foul weather, with fat gray buds opening blue with pale spots. *I. h.* 'Major' has richer colored flowers. *I. foetidissima*, whose red berries are still going strong from autumn, is also an excellent winter bulb.

Above and right: **The tiny, exquisitely marked Reticulata irises put on a late winter and early spring display. *I.* 'J. S. Dijt' (above) and *I.* 'George' (right) are two of the most attractive. Since flowering depends on dry, hot summer conditions, grow them in a rock garden, or a bed with gritty soil. If you want an iris with scent, go for the purple *I. reticulata*. It can also be grown in a pot indoors.**

Winter aconites

Scores of winter aconites (*Eranthis*) will transform areas under deciduous trees and shrubs, creating a great sweep of ground color in late winter. Provided the soil is fertile and moist, they will seed freely. Winter aconites are grown mainly for their exciting cup-shaped flowers, which are bright yellow or white, surrounded by a green ruff. Try them around clumps of hellebores.

Among the best are *Eranthis hyemalis*, $2\frac{1}{2}$ in (6 cm) high, which has goblet-shaped yellow flowers encircled by a frill of bright green leaves. It naturalizes in moist, shady woods in Europe. *E. h.* Cilicia Group is similar but flowers later, and needs reliably hot summers in order to flower prolifically. *E.* Tubergenii Group 'Guinea Gold' is another good choice, and grows slightly taller with a brighter yellow flower against tinged, bronzed leaves. For white-flowering winter aconites, you could try *E. pinnatifida*, 2 in (5 cm) high, but be aware that it does not multiply so rapidly and needs pampering in an alpine house.

Above and right: **In winter, *Eranthis hyemalis*, the winter aconite, covers the ground with an expanse of of pure yellow, the flowers sometimes even peeping through snow and frost.**

The best planting site is beneath deciduous trees where the bulbs will not become desiccated by summer heat. They naturalize easily and combine well with snowdrops and hellebores.

The winter whites

Like the winter aconites, snowdrops (*Galanthus*) are also good naturalizers, with fresh, graceful white flowers that are a welcome sight at the end of winter. *Galanthus reginae-olgae* subsp. *vernalis*, 4 in (10 cm) high, flowers in late winter verging on spring, and is very similar to its autumn cousin *Galanthus reginae-olgae* (*see page 58*). Other snowdrops to try include the *G. nivalis* cultivars, 4 in (10 cm) high. Among the best are *G. n.* 'Flore Pleno', which gives a strong, vivid display of tight double flowers crammed with extra petals; *G. n.* 'Viridapicis', touched with fresh green at the tips of the outer segments; and *G. n.* 'Lady Elphinstone', which has yellow instead of green

markings on its inner tepals. The related *G.* 'Atkinsii' is a first-rate vigorous bulb. It is taller, growing up to 8 in (20 cm), and the flowers are elegantly elongated, marked with green on the tepals.

Some snowdrops may be attractively combined with early-flowering daffodils (*Narcissus*). *Galanthus caucasicus,* which produces large, plump flowers set against bold, broad gray-green leaves, or the slightly earlier-flowering *G. c.* var. *hiemalis* are both perfect partners for the cheerful lemon-yellow *Narcissus* 'Cedric Morris', which reaches 8 in (20 cm) in height.

Of all the winter snowdrops, *Galanthus nivalis* 'Flore Pleno' naturalizes especially well, producing abundant offsets; divide them when the flowers have finished but the foliage is still green, and plant colonies in shady, fertile, moist ground.

If you have a bright, extremely well-drained area, such as a rock garden, try *Puschkinia scilloides*, related to scillas and chionodoxas.

Related to and resembling snowdrops are the snowflakes (*Leucojum*). In addition to those flowering in spring, summer, and autumn, there is a late winter kind, *Leucojum vernum*, 10 in (25 cm) high, with white, green-tipped flowers, which appears at the same time as the snowdrops. Spring snowflakes will thrive in grass, and multiply if left undisturbed, but for a fuller display, try the variety *L. v.* var. *vagneri*, which has two flowers per stem.

If you have a bright, extremely well-drained area in your garden, such as a rock garden, try *Puschkinia scilloides* var. *libanotica*, which is related to scillas and chionodoxas. It is an easy-to-grow late winter bulb that produces a pliable stem, 8 in (20 cm) high, carrying many starry pale blue or white blooms that are prettily marked with darker blue veining.

Far left: **It's easy to get confused by the minute variations between the many different kinds of snowdrop. Far better to plant them in droves, relax, and let them multiply.**

Left: **The starry, silvery-white flowers of *Puschkinia scilloides* var. *libanotica*.**

Above: **The nodding bells of *Leucojum vernum* var. *vagneri* appear by winter's end.**

WINTER GALLERY

Crocus chrysanthus

Height: 2 in (5 cm), spread: 4 cm (1½ in); flowers from late winter to early spring; fully hardy

Vigorous cormous perennial producing globular creamy to bright yellow flowers with a delicate scent, sometimes with attractive maroon speckling or veining on the outside of the petals. Will thrive equally well in the border, in rock gardens, or naturalized in grass. Requires fertile and well-drained soil in full sun.

Cyclamen coum

Height: 2–3 in (5–8 cm), spread: 4 in (10 cm); flowers in midwinter to early spring; fully hardy

Fast-spreading tuberous perennial bearing pink, magenta, or white flowers with a carmine stain around the mouth. Will flower in midwinter in mild areas, later elsewhere. Variable foliage patterning, sometimes attractively mottled silver on green, otherwise shiny and green without any markings. Needs a sheltered site with good drainage and plenty of leafmold, in dappled shade. Naturalizes well.

Eranthis hyemalis (Winter aconite)

Height: 2½ in (6 cm), spread 2 in (5 cm); flowers in late winter to early spring; fully hardy

Brightly colored, low-growing tuberous perennial with cup-shaped bright golden-yellow flowers surrounded by a ruff of bright green foliage. Requires plenty of rich leafmold in light, dappled shade; make sure soil does not dry out over summer. A vigorous grower, it will spread to form large colonies and create a carpet of color if naturalized beneath trees. Pair with snowdrops and cyclamen.

Galanthus nivalis 'Flore Pleno' (Common snowdrop)

Height: 4 in (10 cm), spread 4 in (10 cm); flowers in midwinter; fully hardy

Robust bulbous perennial producing fragile-looking double white flowers with green markings, and green veining inside, dangling from a fine stalk and carried on slender stems. Flowers are surrounded by attractive foliage in the form of dull gray-green narrow strap-shaped leaves. Galanthus are tolerant of many conditions; but prefer fertile soil with added leafmold in light shade; soil must not dry out over summer.

Iris reticulata Hybrids

Height: 5 in (13 cm), spread 2–3 in (5–7.5 cm); flower in late winter and early spring; fully hardy

Gently scented bulbous perennials available in a range of colors from pale blue to purple-red, marked with yellow-orange stripes. The flowers have narrow reflexed petals, giving them a deceptive air of fragility, and the leaves are short at the time of flowering, allowing the blooms to take center stage. There is a large range of cultivars, among which the attractively colored I. 'Cantab', I. 'J. S. Dijt' and I. 'George' are all desirable additions to any garden. Require well-drained, preferably alkaline soil, and an open, sunny site, such as a rock garden or at the front of a bed. Thrive in hot, dry summers, as the bulbs will enjoy a good baking. If left undisturbed for a few years, will grow into sizeable clumps.

Leucojum vernum (Spring snowflake)

Height: 10 in (25 cm), spread: 3 in (8 cm); flowers in winter or early spring; fully hardy

Free-spreading bulbous perennial that is a close relative of the snowdrop family. This is the earliest-flowering Leucojum, appearing in late winter, despite its common name. Has charming and delicate bell-shaped white flowers, tipped with fresh green, held on slender stems above glossy green foliage. Requires fertile, damp ground in partial shade. Excellent for naturalizing.

Puschkinia scilloides var. libanotica

Height: 8 in (20 cm), spread: 2 in (5 cm); flowers in late winter; fully hardy

Small bulbous perennial with a lax stem covered with a dense cluster of star-shaped pale blue flowers marked with darker blue stripes. Thrives in sunny, well-drained, fertile soil with plenty of moisture during the growing season and needs hot, dry summers. Plant beneath shrubs or in a rock garden.

Top left:
***Crocus chrysanthus* 'E. P. Bowles'**

Top right:
***Cyclamen coum* f. *pallidum* 'Album'**

Above left:
Eranthis hyemalis

Above center:
***Galanthus nivalis* 'Flore Pleno'**

Above right:
***Iris* 'Cantab'**

Right:
Leucojum vernum

Opposite page:
Cyclamen coum

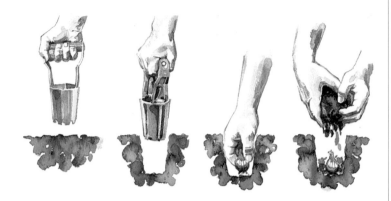

Planting a single bulb Using a bulb planter remove a core of soil. Break up the soil in the bottom. Place the bulb in an upright position into the hole and cover until the soil is at ground level.

Planting depths As a general rule, plant bulbs two to three times deeper than the length of the bulb. Planting bulbs at the incorrect depth can lead to uneven flowering. However, to extend the display of a particular cultivar, try planting half of your bulbs at the correct depth and the other half slightly deeper.

Naturalizing bulbs In order to achieve a random, naturalized look, simply throw a handful of bulbs over the grass and plant them where they have landed

Dividing a bulb Gently pull away any bulblets from around the bulb; these can then be used to grow new plants. Arrange the bulbs in clean shallow trays or boxes and store them in a cool, dry place until it is time for planting in autumn.

care and cultivation

Bulbs are incredibly versatile: they may be planted in beds, naturalized under trees or shrubs or in grass, or grown in rock gardens or containers. Wherever you choose to plant them, bear in mind that bulbs always look best in big, bold groups of the same species or cultivar rather than planted individually or in groups of two or three. One of the dangers of growing bulbs in the garden is that you risk spearing or digging them up. Avoid the problem by planting those that prefer light shade near trees or shrubs where you are less likely to disturb the ground, and where they can also provide valuable color when the trees or shrubs have lost their leaves or are not yet in flower.

Many of the smaller, fussier bulbs require cold, dry winters and hot, dry summers. In cultivation, they need a well-controlled environment to thrive. A rock garden imitates the conditions of the bulbs' natural habitat: a raised, often sunny site with extremely free-draining, gritty, crumbly soil. A position at the foot of a sunny wall can often provide similar conditions.

Planting bulbs

Bulbs may be planted singly or—particularly useful for smaller bulbs—in a large hole in groups. The depth at which the bulb should be planted depends on the size of the bulb. As a general rule, you should dig a hole two to three times deeper than the length of the bulb. In heavy soil, a planting hole that is twice the length of the bulb should be adequate, in lighter conditions, three times the length is more advisable. Break up the firm soil at the bottom of the hole with a hand fork and add compost and a handful of bonemeal to enrich the soil. In heavy soils, add some sharp sand and grit before planting, to ensure better drainage. Position the bulbs in the hole, tips upward. Cover with soil and firm down.

Naturalizing bulbs

Many bulbs increase easily and naturally, spreading to form large "naturalized" areas. The advantage of these bulbs is that they provide an expanse of color in areas that may not otherwise be planted, such as in grass or under trees, and require minimum maintenance on the part of the gardener.

To make the most of areas under deciduous trees or shrubs, plant autumn- and spring-flowering bulbs, such as crocuses or cyclamen. The two lifecycles are complementary: in winter, a deciduous tree or shrub is dormant, so the bulbs can grow happily under the open canopy, which provides light without competing with the tree or shrub for moisture. In summer, the situation is reversed: the tree is growing actively, absorbing moisture, while the bulbs in their dormancy enjoy the partially shaded, relatively dry conditions.

Grass and spring-flowering bulbs complement each other in the same way. The bulbs begin their growth before the grass, then lie dormant over summer, while the grass grows and takes all the moisture it needs without competition from the bulbs. Remember that it is vital to plant tall, vigorous bulbs in tough grass, and smaller bulbs in fine grass. Also, bulbs grown in grass must be allowed to die down naturally before the grass is cut: allow six weeks for daffodils, and four for crocuses. Bulbs increasing by seed, such as *Fritillaria meleagris*, will need an extra three weeks or so to shed their seed. You should also avoid mowing the grass around emerging, autumn-flowering naturalized bulbs in case you scalp the new growth.

When planting large bulbs in grass, use a trowel or a hand-held bulb planter (use the long-handled kind on heavy ground). Like an apple corer, it slips out a plug of soil. Make an individual hole for each bulb, break up the soil in the bottom of the hole, then plant the bulbs in an upright position, covering each one with sod. Alternatively, slice around three sides of the chosen area with a spade, roll back the sod, and plant as above, either singly or, in the case of smaller bulbs, in groups.

Planting bulbs in containers

Growing bulbs in containers enables you to provide bulbs with conditions that meet their exact requirements. This is particularly useful for tender plants, such as the South African bulbs, which can be started off in a cool or gently heated greenhouse, then transferred outside in summer. Woodland bulbs planted in humus-rich potting medium and grit can be positioned in a shady spot. For forced bulbs—those that are specially treated to flower early indoors—pots are also essential.

Select a container—bulbs can be planted in both plastic or clay pots— and drill drainage holes if necessary. Place shards of broken pottery or pebbles at the base of the pot, then a layer of potting medium. For bulbs requiring very good drainage, you will need to add plenty of grit to the potting medium. Plant bulbs at about three times the depth of the bulb, each one a bulb's width apart. Cover with potting medium, leaving a $\frac{1}{2}$ in (1 cm) gap below the rim of the pot. Repot annually with fresh potting medium before the bulbs start regrowth. For bulbs that require a hot, dry summer dormancy, water occasionally; summer growers should be watered regularly.

Routine care

Bulbs have their own energy supplies, so as a general rule, do not feed them on planting. With most bulbs wait until after flowering, but before the leaves fade, then apply a balanced fertilizer to help boost energy for next year's display. Always keep fresh manure away from bulbs, they do not react well to it, although well-rotted manure is advisable in advance of planting. Potted bulbs need a tomato fertilizer when in bud. For bulbs growing in grass, give a potash-high tomato feed to encourage flower production, and nitrogen to encourage leafy growth.

Dividing bulbs

Some bulbs multiply at such a rate that they become congested, and flowering diminishes. If this occurs, dig up the bulbs just before they come into growth, and divide them into smaller sections. The new growth might take two years to flower. Snowdrops (*Galanthus*) and aconites (*Aconitum*) are exceptions, being best divided immediately after flowering, when they are "in the green." If they are divided while in growth, make sure the clumps are well watered when they are replaced.

Pests and diseases

Given the right conditions, you should have few problems with bulbs; poor growing conditions, however, can lead to bulb blindness, when the bulb produces foliage but no flowers, and increased susceptibility to disease. Prevention is easier than cure, so use a systemic fungicide dip when the bulbs are dormant. Below is a list of some of the pests and diseases that affect bulbous plants, as well as ways of treating them.

● Aphids disfigure leaves and stunt growth. The larvae of the narcissus fly, which affects daffodils as well as other plants, eats and destroys the center of the bulb. Mounding soil over the bulb, around the stem base, as flowers fade, helps seal out the flies. Spray at the first sign of attack or as a prevention with an appropriate insecticide.

● Caterpillars attack the leaves and flowers of bulbs. Collect up and dispose of them, apply insecticide or use a biological control.

● Earwigs eat the leaves of some bulbs in summer, particularly those of dahlias. Trap them in inverted pots filled with dried grass, stuck on stakes. Destroy the contents daily.

● Ink spot disease can affect Reticulata irises. Diseased bulbs have black crusty patches on their outer scales. Destroy any affected bulbs.

● Lily disease causes small, red-brown, oval-shapes patches of fungus to appear on the leaves of lilies. Cut off and burn any infected growth and treat with a systemic fungicide.

● Mealybugs tend to be a greater problem in the greenhouse than in the open garden, congregating in inaccessible places such as at the base of a leaf, stunting or distorting growth. For biological control, ladybirds will help to control their numbers; otherwise, use an insecticide.

● Red lily beetles and their larvae destroy the leaves of lilies and fritillaries. Pick off when seen and spray with an insecticide.

● Red spider mites affect the leaves of bulbous plants. They thrive in hot, dry conditions, so mist foliage with water and do not allow pots to dry out.

● Rust causes bright orange or dark brown marks on leaves. Remove any affected stems and treat with a fungicide spray.

● Slugs and snails eat bulbs, leaves, and stems of bulbous plants, mainly at night. Leave bowls of beer out at night for them to drown in or use slug pellets; spread ashes on the ground or gravel around a plant; or use an insidious nematode called *Phasmarhabditis hermaphrodita*.

● Thrips attack gladioli, sucking out the sap and leading to discoloration and destruction of the plant. Dust the bulbs with fungicide when dormant.

● Tulip fire rots new growth of tulips before flowering. To prevent it from occurring, grow tulips on a new site every third year, and remove the foliage and petals after they have died down naturally.

● Vine weevils attack bulbs in containers. Pick them off when they emerge at night, and use a nematode, *Heterohabditis megidis*, that can be watered onto the soil in late summer. Be warned—it is not active in dry soils, or when the temperature drops below 57°F (14°C).

● Viruses affect all bulbous plants. Severely diseased plants should always be destroyed. Try to choose only new stock that is certified as being free of viruses. Spray plants regularly to keep aphids at bay.

Picture credits

The publishers would like to thank the photographers and garden owners for allowing us to reproduce the photographs on the following pages:

Endpapers J. Harpur,1; M. Harpur; 2 J. Harpur; 3 J. Harpur; 4–5 M. Harpur/Dr and Mrs Chris Grey-Wilson, Suffolk; 6 J. Harpur/Chiffchaffs, Dorset; 6–7 J. Harpur/Wollerton Old Hall, Shropshire; 8 J. Harpur/design Michael Balston, Patney, Wiltshire; 8–9 J. Harpur/design Xa Tollemache, RHS Chelsea Flower Show 1997; 9 M. Harpur/RHS Wisley, Surrey; 10 J. Harpur/Dower House, Barnsley, Gloucestershire; 11 left J. Harpur; 11 right J. Harpur; 12 J. Harpur; 13 J. Harpur/Beth Chatto Gardens, Essex; 14 J. Harpur/Writtle College, Essex; 15 above J. Harpur; 15 below J. Harpur/Dolwen, Powys; 16 M. Harpur/Chiffchaffs, Dorset; 17 left J. Harpur; 17 right J. Harpur; 18 left J. Harpur/RHS Wisley, Surrey; 18 right J. Harpur; 19 J. Harpur/Writtle College, Essex; 20 J. Harpur; 21 J. Harpur; 22 J. Harpur; 23 J. Harpur/Longwood Gardens, Philadelphia; 24 left John Glover/Garden Picture Library; 24 right Clive Nichols; 25 left Densey Clyne/Garden Picture Library; 25 right John Glover/Garden Picture Library; 26–27 J. Harpur/RHS Wisley, Surrey; 27 J. Harpur/Dolwen, Powys; 28 J. Harpur; 29 clockwise from top left J. Harpur; J. Harpur/ Beth Chatto Gardens, Essex; J. Harpur; J. Harpur; J. Harpur; J. Harpur; 30 J. Harpur; 31 left J. Harpur; 31 right J. Harpur; 32 J. Harpur/RHS Rosemoor, Devon; 33 J. Harpur; 34 J. Harpur/ Manor House, Bledlow, Buckinghamshire; 35 left M. Harpur/ Beth Chatto Gardens, Essex; 35 right J. Harpur/Barnsley House, Gloucestershire; 36–37 J. Harpur/RHS Wisley, Surrey; 37 above J. Harpur; 37 below J. Harpur; 38 M. Harpur/Dr and Mrs Chris Grey-Wilson, Suffolk; 39 left J. Harpur/design Linda Teague, California; 39 right J. Harpur; 40 M. Harpur/Holkham Hall, Wells-next-the-Sea, Norfolk; 41 left J. Harpur/RHS Wisley, Surrey; 41 right J. Harpur; 42 J. Harpur/RHS Wisley, Surrey; 43 J. Harpur/Scott Arboretum, Pennsylvania; 44 left J. Harpur; 44 right J. Harpur/Edinburgh Royal Botanic Garden; 45 J. Harpur; 46 J. Harpur; 47 left J. Harpur; 47 right J. Harpur/ Villa Ramsdal, Chelmsford, Essex; 48 J. Harpur; 49 clockwise from top left M. Harpur; J. Harpur; J. Harpur/design Linda Teague, California; J. Harpur; J. Harpur/design Linda Teague, California; J. Harpur; 50–51 J. Harpur; 52 J. Harpur/ Anglesey Abbey, Lode, Cambridgeshire; 53 J. Harpur/Great Dixter, East Sussex; 54 J. Harpur/design Dan Hinkley, Seattle; 55 left J. Harpur/RHS Wisley, Surrey; 55 right J. Harpur/RHS Wisley, Surrey; 56 left J. Harpur; 56 right J. Harpur/Beth Chatto Gardens, Essex; 57 J. Harpur/Great Dixter, East Sussex; 58 left H. Rice/Garden Picture Library/Beth Chatto Gardens, Essex; 58 right H. Rice/Garden Picture Library; 59 J. Harpur; 60–61 J. Harpur; 61 above J. Harpur; 61 below Andrew Lawson/Tintinhull, Somerset; 62 J. Harpur/RHS Wisley, Surrey; 62–63 J. Harpur/Great Dixter, East Sussex; 64 J. Harpur/RHS Wisley, Surrey; 65 clockwise from top left Andrew Lawson; J. S. Sira/ Garden Picture Library; M. Harpur; J. Harpur; J. Harpur; J. Harpur; 66 R. Estall/Garden Picture Library; 67 J. S. Sira/ Garden Picture Library/Polesden Lacey, Surrey; 68 left J. Harpur; 68–69 J. Harpur; 69 J. Harpur; 70 left J. Harpur; 70 right J. Harpur; 71 left J. Harpur; 71 right J. Harpur/Barnsley House, Gloucestershire; 72 J. Harpur/ Painswick Rococo Garden, Gloucestershire; 73 left J. Harpur/ Beth Chatto Gardens, Essex; 73 right J. Harpur; 74 J. Harpur; 75 clockwise from top left J. Harpur/Writtle College, Essex; J. Harpur; J. Harpur; J. Harpur; J. Harpur; J. Harpur; 80 M. Harpur/Chenies Manor, Bucks.